P9-DEK-410

FACE TO FACE TO FACE

An Experiment in Intimacy

edited by
Gordon Clanton
and Chris Downing

E. P. DUTTON & CO., INC.   NEW YORK   1975

GARDNER WEBB COLLEGE LIBRARY

LIBRARY OF CONGRESS CATALOGING IN PUBLICATION DATA

Clanton, Gordon, comp.
Face to face to face: an experiment in intimacy.

Contains journals and autobiographical sketches of
three individuals with commentary by the editors.
Bibliography: p.
1. Marriage—United States. 2. Intimacy (Psychology) 3. Lesbianism. 4. Group sex. I. Downing,
Chris, joint comp. II. Title.
HQ734.C566 1975   301.42'23   74-22047

Copyright © 1975 by Gordon Clanton and Chris Downing.
All rights reserved. Printed in the U.S.A.
First Edition

10 9 8 7 6 5 4 3 2 1

No part of this publication may be reproduced or transmitted in any form or by
any means, electronic or mechanical, including photocopy, recording, or any information storage and retrieval system now known or to be invented, without permission in writing from the publisher, except by a reviewer who wishes to quote brief
passages in connection with a review written for inclusion in a magazine, newspaper
or broadcast.

Published simultaneously in Canada by Clarke, Irwin & Company
Limited, Toronto and Vancouver
ISBN: 0-525-10208-6

HQ
734
C566
1975

G

$6.94

B+T

8-2-76

For
Jan
and
George

The editors wish to acknowledge their deep personal appreciation to Rich and Amy and Karen for their cooperation in this project and to Walter Blass, Juris Jurjevics, Margie Kahn and Joanne Sheitelman for theirs.

CONTENTS

PREFACE

In the summer of 1970, a young married couple, whom we call Rich and Amy, opened their home to a single woman, whom we call Karen. The three committed themselves to what they described as a group marriage. Each considered himself/herself married to the other two. They lived together for six months, during which time they attempted to share everything: living space, money, psychic support, sexual expression, and long-range plans.

Each kept a journal, recording experiences and feelings as they happened. These journals are the core of this book.

Many of the experiences recorded here are not typical; they are not part of the behavioral repertoire of the average American. Included in these first-person accounts are descriptions of and references to masturbation, adultery, lesbian activities, experiences with psychedelic drugs, and group nudity and group sex among intimate friends and among total strangers. Despite this, the reader who is looking for the pornographic or the sensational will be disappointed. Rich and Amy and Karen kept journals to serve their own needs, not to titillate or entertain.

We met Amy and Rich and Karen in the course of our ongoing study of changing forms of intimate association. Our focus is on various forms of *consensual adultery* or *comarital sex*, that is, extramarital sex with the knowledge and consent of the spouse and in the context of mutual commitment to the preservation of the marriage bond.

Our interviews with Rich and Amy and Karen afforded us a close look at one type of consensual adultery, the group marriage, *and* gave us glimpses of the swinging subculture and other kinds of comarital sex. Later, as we worked through the journals they made available to us, we came to feel that these accounts provided a unique access to the day-by-day working out of an experiment in emotional and sexual intimacy, an experiment that takes place at the growing edge of today's search for those human arrangements and institutions which make life pleasurable and meaningful. The fullness of these first-person accounts allows a rare opportunity for a close look at a phenomenon usually reported only superficially. Also, a threesome is the simplest alternative form to study; it raises most of the questions pertinent to larger groups, but it is simple enough so that we can grasp what is going on.

When Karen came to live with them, Rich and Amy were in their late twenties. They had known each other for eight years. They had lived together for five of these and had been married for four. They shared a long-standing commitment to very liberal sexual values. Each was open to the other having sexual experiences outside their marriage, and each had acted on that freedom many times, always with the knowledge and approval of the spouse. Their extramarital sexual experiences had occurred both at swinging parties and in the context of close friendships. These activities seem to have generated very little jealousy or interpersonal conflict.

The outward appearance they present to the world is fairly conservative. Both were in graduate school during the academic year 1970–71. Rich's hair is not overly long by contemporary standards. He and Amy dress simply but neatly. Their suburban home is comfortable and tastefully furnished. There is nothing in their public demeanor to suggest that they are hippies or political radicals.

Karen, too, is essentially conventional in dress, grooming, and self-presentation. Also in her late twenties, she was an old friend of Rich's but had met Amy only in passing. In the spring of 1970, Karen was working as a secretary in another part of the country. Her relationship with the man with whom she was living was unsatisfactory.

We present the journals out of the conviction that ours is a transitional time with regard to the ways in which intimate relationships are formed and maintained. The questions Rich and Amy and Karen wrestle with in these pages are questions that perplex many people and will perplex many more. Perhaps a close look at a single experiment is one avenue to a better understanding of the whole range of social phenomena of which this group marriage is part. And perhaps an empathetic look at such a venture can be of value to individuals curious about their own needs and limits.

We have edited the journals with a light hand. We have changed the names of all persons and places in order to disguise identities. We have omitted some material and done some rearranging, but we have made very few changes in wording. Each writer's distinctive style is part of the story. We feel that there is considerable value in noting the similarities and differences among the three accounts of particular experiences. In some cases, we have reordered the journal material in order to facilitate this kind of revealing comparison.

The careful reader of these journals may find them irritating in spots (as we did) because each writer has his or her

annoying traits. Such faults, however, do not detract substantially from the value of the journals as social docu-
ments.

The book has no heroes. We are presenting these charac-
ters, not so that the reader will like or dislike them, but so
that he can learn from their experiences. That Rich often
comes on as a male chauvinist, that each of the three on
occasion seems to be posturing, that they pay little attention
to rendering the flavor of the pragmatic details of everyday
living—these peculiarities are part of how it was.

It is our hope that each reader will form his own evalua-
tion of the experiences described here. We have added to the
first-person accounts an interpretive essay in which we explore the human dynamics of this group marriage and its
relationship to the larger social context in which it occurred
and in which we all live. But our editorial commentary is not
intended to serve as a substitute for careful reading and
thoughtful reflection.

Yet, a word of caution is perhaps in order here. It may
not always be appropriate to judge new forms by old crite-
ria. There is a tendency to see *permanence* as an essential
property of a successful marriage and therefore to judge
various alternative living arrangements unsuccessful because they are short-lived. The time for a reconsideration of
this way of thinking may be at hand. It seems to be a mark
of the times that increasing numbers of people, especially
the young, go through a series of personal conversions in
the course of their lives and so require a whole sequence of
different social and emotional contexts. Some contemporary social thinkers have suggested that the future will belong to "protean man," to those who can identify problems,
invent temporary institutional systems that solve them, and
disband or discard those systems when new needs arise.
Whether or not we can endure the turbulence of protean or
temporary marriage is yet to be determined, but perhaps
we can at least tentatively endorse a favorite text of Rich's

taken from the psychologist Sidney Jourard: "The family structure for the emerging age cannot be prescribed or described in advance—only invented."

September 30, 1974

Gordon Clanton
Chris Downing

SELF SKETCHES

These brief statements were composed by
Amy, Rich, and Karen late in September
1970 at the request of the editors

AMY

Rich and I have always had a very solid, deep, secure, growing relationship. We have grown closer together in the eight years that we have known each other (four of them married) than most people probably do in a lifetime. We know each other very well because we are committed to being open with each other. Our knowledge of each other is limited only by our self-deception; for what we do not know of ourselves, we cannot share except as the other person is able to perceive it from without. That is, of course, one of the ways in which we increase our self-knowledge: through reflection by the other. Knowing ourselves better and knowing each other better is a never-ending, dynamic, satisfying adventure. Having this commitment seems to result in a spin-off effect on our other interpersonal relations. We come to have higher expectations of them and place higher demands on them for openness, closeness, and intimacy. For the most part, we are disappointed. When there are people who are exceptions to this, we value them highly and feel very strongly about them.

We would go far out of our way for them, and have on occasion. Karen is one of these people, and circumstances made it possible for us to attempt to develop that friendship into an even deeper relationship. I suppose marriage (living together with intent of permanency) is one way of increasing intimacy with another and at the same time a logical outgrowth of increased intimacy. That's the basic motivation in a nutshell.

Going further and getting into more specific, less overarching motives and desires, let me just tumble a number of them out.

I have more than enough of almost everything. Thus, I can share without being deprived. For example, Rich has a higher need for companionship than I do; thus, if our marriage were expanded, his desires and needs for companionship would be even more fully met while, at the same time, I could have a little bit more time to myself, which I sometimes feel a very real need for. Rich has a stronger sex drive than I do in that he wants to make love more often than I do; thus, to have Karen join us would allow him to better meet his sexual needs while, at the same time, allowing me to seek more my own level of sexual satisfaction. I hate to reject his sexual approaches, but I am not always able to accept them, and I feel badly.

I have come to feel in the last few years a lack of female companionship. Always, in high school and college, I had close girl friends to share with. But I haven't for some time now; there has been no other girl that I would get together with and do things with and just sit and chat with. And there are little things that girls tend to see in the same way and understand that guys, even as close and understanding a guy as Rich, just don't because they've got a different perspective. Couple that with a developing bisexuality, and the idea of having Karen here to share with appealed to me. Not only could I have the companionship of another girl but hopefully the sexual companionship of another girl as well. What more could anyone want than to have the desire for both close male companionship and close female companionship met at home, in one's own family?

I did not know Karen very well, but I trusted Rich, and he thought we would like each other and get along living together. Incidentally, Karen was the first girl that Rich had had an affair with that I felt no jealousy toward. This happened while he and I were getting to know each other in Los Angeles; I knew about it at the time but did not know her then. I first met Karen three weeks after we were married in 1966, when we got to Palo Alto, and my first reaction on meeting her was a combination of relief that I did not feel jealous and the feeling, "Here's someone I could like more than anyone I've met in a long time."

So we corresponded, the three of us, by letter and by taped letter, and disclosed and discussed and questioned. Our feelings for each other grew, and we made the commitment to join our lives.

It was scary. The relationship between Rich and Karen was in no way a threat to me in terms of my relationship with Rich; I have a very basic security there. What scared me was how I would be able to hold up my end with Karen: Would I really like her? Would she really like me? Would I be able to be open, really open, with her? Would a sexual relationship work out between us? What if she was not interested in relating sexually with me? I was afraid that if a sexual relationship didn't work out between us, I would feel tension and would feel that things didn't balance out in the three-way relationship.

I feared that Rich and I would miss our privacy. We were not used to someone else being around all the time. This had been a problem when we had spent one to two months each summer in Colorado with Rich's parents. As much as we both love them and enjoy their company (I enjoy spending much more time with them than with my own parents), after we had been there awhile, we would come to feel a need for more privacy—to make love with each other without worrying about making noise, to talk openly without worrying about someone else hearing, just to be together alone, not to have to run on someone else's schedule, etcetera. I was afraid —and so was Rich—that we would talk more openly with each other when Karen was not around and feel inhibited in conversing on various things when she was around. This would be exhibited to us in our breaking off conversations when she would enter the room or by seeking each other out alone to bring things up, probably problems. For the most part, this hasn't happened, and it was a relief and a satisfaction that it didn't.

There were societal risks involved also. I would have to deal with the question of my parent's knowledge and reaction eventually if it worked out. Our professional careers could possibly suffer if our personal life were known, and a family of three is not exactly an unobtrusive thing. Besides, we don't like the idea of hiding something we believe in and feel good about and are proud of, especially when that thing is a person. There are innumerable future obstacles that we may encounter, a lot of them from without.

Mostly, we just want to grow closer—to Karen and to each other.

RICH

To state the matter in purely emotional terms, I simply found myself loving two women, of similar temperament, demeanor, and character (but with interesting differences), who, as I appraised it, had a liking and a need for one another. There was a small but nagging kind of conflict involved but no consideration of substituting one for the other, that is, of leaving Amy to be with Karen. I also found myself intellectually curious about the effects such a combination experience-experiment might have on each of us personally. What transformations might be forthcoming, and what kind of a group might we be for ourselves and for others? To me, it also seemed socially daring, sexually interesting, and a personal challenge. Could I, even on short terms and with modest commitments legally and socially, live happily with two women as well or better than one?

A group marriage, as I conceived it, held ever so much more promise for personal development, companionship, sexual variety, and differentiation in style and identity and family function than the ordinary model of the conventional, or even the unconventional, marital dyad. Abstractly, I could see no necessary flaws in the idea, only personal and/or interpersonal failures in relating to others. This is not to say I or we did not anticipate problem areas. Indeed, in the months prior to our actual physical and social coming together, I took pains to discuss these in person with Amy and by letter and tape with Karen. I also encouraged them to communicate expectations, fears, soft or sore spots, etcetera, with one another.

I saw a group marriage as providing levels and types of intimacy which I desired and felt capable of that are not usually found among social peer groups, even of the deviant sort where such intimacy is lauded, such as swinging. I had experienced both good and bad aspects of swinging, and I found it, after a period of emotional digestion and intellectual reflection, inadequate but pleasant and unthreatening. The type of sexual freedom suggested by both casual and sustained involvements with other couples pointed the way to deeper and more rewarding types of relationships. Specifically, I felt—both abstractly as an academician and concretely as a person—that the greater the number of personal relationships with the greatest and deepest level of commitment, intimacy, affection, and love an individual could participate in, the more social and the more mature the person. A group marriage, especially with two women I already knew and loved, whom I desired and found interesting, seemed to fit this very well. A serious why-not-try-it? attitude emerged.

There is also a practical aspect to this: Three (or more) persons could more easily pursue their individual interests within the framework of a family *if* they could achieve or approach the levels of trust and intimacy and interest already achieved by the preexisting dyad. It meant, as I saw it, a relief for *both* Amy and Karen from domestic chores and roles which they each perform well but which they each wished to transcend. I also saw them providing one another with a beneficial type of companionship which I as a male could not fulfill. I saw them as potential friends and lovers, *sisters* in the best sense of the term. It also provided an avenue for their specifically homosexual feelings, since I knew that they each found the other sexually attractive. They are both bisexual, and this not only intrigued me and could serve as a source of arousal but also provided a nonthreatening way for me to explore various sexual feelings in myself. In a word, I felt they were ahead of me on that score but that they had a great deal to learn and unlearn themselves.

I saw the advantages of the emotional and domestic support and felt that I could get much encouragement from each of them for various demanding tasks I had set myself, thereby effecting a real mutual exchange of emotional services. I saw myself playing a therapeutic role for each of them, inasmuch as I found Karen to have the same kind of confidence and self-esteem difficulties I had discovered over a period of time in Amy. I saw in them much personal potential and saw myself aiding and abetting its realization.

There were, of course, risks involved, serious ones. Such a deviant adventure could produce a whirlpool of unmanageable problems into which I might be pulled, with no way out emotionally even if the threesome dissolved socially and physically. It would leave permanent effects, I knew. One major risk was the possible alteration and/or destruction of the emotional relationship between Amy and me. Could we, as a twosome, withstand the pressures created by deviance and nonconformity. This was the biggest risk but also seemed one most worth taking, since even if we failed as a threesome, it *could* bring us even closer together. We would have withstood an adventure, which for us as intellectuals held special interest. Was a new social form really possible?

The second major risk was simply that of falling in love and being deeply involved and committed to a person, a risk I had already run with Amy with apparent success after over seven years. Being involved means being exposed, and being exposed raises the possibility of being hurt, also shamed, disappointed, ridiculed. One countervailing thought was that if I failed with Karen, Amy and I could console one another. So that even though we might be risking some elements of our preexisting marriage, we had the consolation of each other if we failed. Karen was not risking a marriage, but at the same time, her risk, independent of such a factor, was individually larger, for she would have no one to fall back on unless something developed for her in the meantime.

Another risk was with our friends. Many of them were in some way social and/or sexual deviants and were, on the whole, well educated; but there was a fear that many of them were pseudononconformists in spite of this and would either not know how to relate to us *as a threesome* or would not, for some reason, probably some fear of their own, want to. We are attempting to make new friends as a threesome in a fairly deliberate way. One note: Some persons seem to tune out or not take seriously the fact that we are a group and therefore see me as a married swinger with an extra female appended for various pleasures. This I take as a projection from some males. They do not see that I also deeply love and feel responsible for both Amy and Karen.

A fourth risk was with our families, especially parents. I told my parents our intentions, and they were initially shocked and feared some sort of breakup. They were surprised by Amy's explanations and acceptance, and when Karen joined us in the Rockies in July, they were—after some tense moments—impressed. I do believe my father was secretly envious, but by the time we left (only two days later), all seemed well, and they embraced and encouraged each of us. Amy's father knows nothing of the threesome. Amy's mother knows there is "a girl" living with us, on the pretexts of her being a previous friend needing a place to live on her return to Palo Alto and of us living in a larger, more expensive house. I am concerned about what her response may be if and when she discovers the truth. As for my other relatives (I have no brothers or sisters), I couldn't care what they think as long as they don't ridicule or harass my parents, and I don't think they will ever know because there is no reason or opportunity to disclose the matter.

There are some other smaller risks. One concerns my professional standing. The second is the potential legal problems such a marriage might raise. We would be harassed, even prosecuted; but it is unlikely, and we can take steps to avoid such complications. Nonetheless, I resent a society in which such private arrangements are illegal and must to some extent, be suppressed.

KAREN

I met Rich in a class I was taking at UCLA. We saw each other a few times, and I was surprised to learn he was living with his girl friend and *still* interested in seeing me. And what was even more puzzling, she knew he was seeing me and growing to care for me, and it was okay with her.

My knowledge of Amy was via Rich. She called for him a couple of times at my apartment, and I think I saw her at the beach once, but there was no real contact until we were all in the Bay Area. We began getting acquainted when I moved to Dallas, thus eliminating further face-to-face getting to know one another till I returned to the Bay Area. During the time I was in Dallas, we (Rich and I, with occasional notes from Amy) corresponded fairly frequently and the last year to year and a half very frequently. The last six to ten months, there were numerous tapes from Rich and Amy (one from me; I'm shy with a tape recorder).

It's difficult to nail down a precise day, month, etcetera, when we began thinking of group marriage. I suppose if you need an incident, it was a phone call I made to Rich and Amy from Dallas. I was crying and upset and terribly unhappy, and they sent me money to get back to San Francisco and extended an invitation to stay with them until I found a job, etcetera. For reasons I won't go into in detail, I decided to stay in Dallas but nevertheless appreciated their offer and saw the implications and possible repercussions, neither of which distressed me. I felt good and loved and wanted.

As time drew nearer for me to return to San Francisco, we began discussing my breakup with Brian (some time in the offing) and again the offer of their home to come to until I could get an apartment, etcetera.

I made a tape to Rich and Amy, but for some reason they couldn't get anything from it except a word here and there. So on a chance feeling, Rich called me and asked if I'd like to live with them, and I immediately said yes.

We then began many discussions via taped letter and occasional phone call regarding our new arrangement. What an exciting adventure. We discussed all sorts of pros and cons, made various disclosures, etcetera. I can't remember at the moment who first asked me "Why?", but I recall being at a momentary loss for words. It all appeared so obvious to me.

Basically, I suppose I would say I love Rich, but I can't give that simple an answer. I do indeed love Rich, and then there was the possibility-probability that I would love Amy, too. The advantages of a threesome over a twosome seem quite clear. I had never had a close, close girl friend, even in high school, and Amy and I seemed to be very much alike according to Rich. We discovered it for ourselves as time went on.

Why does *anyone* want to get married? For love, for companionship, for sharing. Well, all these still apply; they're simply expanded. I've always admired Rich and Amy's respect for their marriage and each other. Their freer, no-deception marriage was infinitely more appealing than marriages with each partner hiding something (or someone) from the other. I never dreamed I'd be a part of it, but now it all seems perfectly natural.

I also feel a need to complete my education, but even more than that to never *stop* my education, the personal inner growth, and Rich and Amy have always epitomized that growth to me. Rich is a very stimulating man (mentally and sexually) to be around, and I had hoped Amy would be, too. I'm so lucky; she is!

We also discussed risks involved in our new relationship. I felt one of the biggest was for Amy and me. There was the possibility we *wouldn't* hit it off. Two women in one house —that could be courting disaster, but in our case it wasn't. Amy and I get along beautifully, and we're becoming closer and meshing together better all the time.

Perhaps the largest risk for each of us is if our marriage doesn't work out. The effects of a failure could be devastating, far more so than in a two-person marriage. I can't conceive of us not together. I would feel so incomplete in a two-person marriage now.

THE JOURNALS

AMY

Thursday, July 9 It's our first night in the house. We came together six days ago at Rich's parents' home and spent three days together there, and then Karen and I had a wonderful three-day drive across country while Rich flew to San Francisco. But now it's different; now we're alone together in what is to be our home.

Lying closely and resting together, soaking up each other's presence, I felt things becoming sexual and felt it was time for me to opt out and allow Karen and Rich time to be together as two, which they had not yet had. Saying so, and as it was the second day of my period, I left and retired to a hot bubble bath—champagne bubble bath, one of our arrival gifts from Rich. Getting into the tub, I began to have a fear seep into my good feelings about their sharing and my departure. I was afraid I would hear the sounds of Karen's arousal and be jealous and hurt because I had not been able to induce those sounds of joy. The faucets of the tub dripped, and I turned them very hard to stop the sound so that I could hear what I feared. Almost immediately, I heard such extreme sounds of glory emanating from Karen, I ached inside and felt sadly aroused by them myself. How I want to please her so! I don't know what to do about my feelings except to comfort myself with thoughts of patience and her love and thoughtfulness, but I know I will take them hot towels when they have exhausted themselves and I finish my bath. Her sounds continue almost steadily, crying with beautiful release and newfound pleasure, laughing with joy, and straining and moaning with active response. I love them both so. And I am glad he is pleasing her and she him; someday *I* will, and I will feel very proud and happy.

My wife! What a strange concept. I always thought I would *be* one, never that I would *have* one. One can project the complexities and irregularities of social introductions, visualizing a scene in which one says to an outside party, "This is my husband, and this is my wife!"

Friday, July 10 Second day in the house. Karen read what I had written last night, although she hasn't said so to either of us. I left my note pad in the bathroom partially sticking out from under a magazine so that one or both of them would find it without knowing I hoped they would. It seemed a good way of sharing those feelings which it seemed were not subject to (or appropriate for) resolution by discussion. I could have brought them up, but there was no immediate way to change them by doing so.

Karen came out of the bathroom quietly crying with feelings but left her feelings subsumed under the explanation and interpretation of a general emotional overload and catharsis. Soon she retired to the bedroom, worn out, and Rich followed to probe her tears and feelings, and they drifted into lovemaking again. I sat in the black fur chair in the living room, feeling lonely, open, and defenseless and determined to stay that way even though it hurt because it also felt good not to hide and cover up and scapegoat and rationalize and blame.

Every cry she made cut through me like a knife, and I clutched my stomach in pain. Again, not because she was with him and he with her, but for feeling incapable of pleasing her as Rich does. On reflecting, I realized and accepted that I would probably never be able to make her feel like he does. I shall learn to please her in a different way, with a different kind of intensity, as females please females.

They both came out to me afterward, and we held each other and rested quietly together, and I felt comforted and included once again. At first, Rich had come out, and I waited and waited, dreading as each moment passed that she was going to go to bed and to sleep without communicating with me. Not only did she not do that, but she put on the openwork vest I had crocheted for her before her arrival to barely cover her beautifully while we had a bedtime snack. It was the first time she had worn it. I felt touched by her thoughtfulness.

I have come to realize that part of what I have been feeling is due to having had Karen to myself for three days during the trip back, and what I'm having to learn now is to share her. Rich and I have already learned to share. Now I must learn it again with Karen, as each of us must learn it with each other.

Today was a day of acclimating and of "Christmas." Karen, our early riser and morning person, got up early and had some time to herself, which is good for settling into new surroundings. It was a lazy day, getting to know each other more and opening all of Karen's boxes and examining and exclaiming over their contents, which will soon be arranged around the house and become a part of it. I napped before dinner, giving Rich and Karen time together again. They made love and then afterward came together to wake me from my nap, one on one side of me and one on the other.

For the first time, we made love together as three, in a relaxed, easy way, not intense, but like intercourse the second time in close succession tends to be, comfortable and known and already partially satisfied. Rich asked me after they woke me if I had masturbated this morning when I got up and informed me I was the only one who hadn't. Karen suggested maybe it had to do with their having made love last night and my not. I confessed with a laugh that I had masturbated before falling asleep for my nap. I had not wanted to listen for their sounds.

I am in the tub again before bedtime, and I can once again hear their loving sounds, this time from the bedroom. And this time it does not hurt. Probably it is because this afternoon I was included in their loving, though I did not take an active part or attempt to satisfy Karen on my own but only tried to augment in little ways her response to Rich and her pleasure. I feel good and very happy, but shy and holding back some. I will be glad when my period is over and I can participate fully.

Our tastes are fantastically alike; we have decided it's kind of eerie! So many things we have are the same, like bathroom towels and dinner dishes and some candleholders which have always been a joke between Rich and me because the candles always run over the side. What is not the same complements and blends or is something I've wanted or liked and desired but not yet gotten, like earthenware dishes. Tomorrow we see how two women get along together in the grocery store.

I've noticed Karen makes me feel more feminine. I wonder if it's because she's so feminine or simply the presence of another female in my home environment. I haven't really had a close girl friend since high school, evidently a common state; Karen says she hasn't either. We share girl things and reinforce feminine feelings. I've missed that since marriage, and now I can enjoy it again, but this time with the addition of an overt sexual component.

I also feel like I'm out to stay. No more hiding from myself and other people, no more difference between the outside and the inside, the presented front and the real thing. No more running around so full of self-consciousness and insecurities. Perhaps once real openness and transparency transcend the crucial difference barrier between the two-person and three-person group, it is more readily expandable. Perhaps it can become a way of interacting with the world for me.

What do you do when there's three in the bed and the one in the middle's the only one who's too warm?

RICH

Saturday, July 11 On July 4, 1970, my life underwent what I think is a most significant change, a change akin to graduating from college, choosing a career, starting a business, or choosing a life partner. It is so very much like the latter that it may be just that. Only in this instance, I had already made such a choice, an enviable one; and now a new woman has entered my life, my home, and is taking a place she already had in my heart.

The three of us—Amy, Karen, and I—hope and intend to initiate and sustain a three-person *group marriage.* In current vernacular, it is a threesome, or as the more sophisticated French label it, a ménage à trois, though I hope to avoid the ordinarily vulgar connotations that attach to these labels.

We intend that our marriage shall be *experimental* in the sense that we are attempting a new form of marital life, one not restricted to dyadic intimacy and communication. It shall be *open* socially, sexually, and emotionally in the sense that we are each free to experience, to explore, and to satisfy our impulses and our needs as they arise with each other in our peculiar triadic way or with other persons outside our little group, as we individually see fit. And it shall be committed to principles of *growth* and *maturation* as we as individuals see them. On the other side of the issue, we shall attempt to avoid the usual legal, social, and religious restrictions and sanctions of conventional marriage relationships.

This is indeed a tall order. But it makes no sense to do as many hip, mod, and faddish persons do: attempt to create a radically different life-style only to fetter it with the same restrictions associated with the institution of marriage of the past. It may seem too black and white to some persons, but either we are free to grow and expand and better ourselves, or we are not. Halfhearted commitments are often worse than no commitment at all. We may be pushing ourselves beyond our limits, but it is a compelling experiment nonetheless, and my curiosity is almost as high as my concern for the outcome.

The decision to live together was one not easily or lightly arrived at, one even less easily accomplished. Clearly, it may set us apart, sometimes in painful ways, from other persons and perhaps from each other.

We had resolved previously that each of us would keep a journal, though the detailed plan of our entries and how and when we share them has not yet been settled. I only hope that they each contain our candid and reflective thoughts, our reactions, our aspirations, our expectations, our fears, our disappointments, and our individual perspectives and interpretations of our collective experiences. Most recent efforts (mostly fictional and/or pornographic accounts) to convey the realities of group marriage seem to focus on the sexual deviation implicit in such arrangements and tend to give us prejudicial descriptions of the personalities that might be drawn to them. I have some hope that we may avoid that pitfall.

Since I am a philosopher by both temperament and training, my account will likely be more abstract, something which may be more of a defect than an asset, since we are after both immediacy of emotional feeling *and* insights and reflections. But the girls will likely make up for this with their wonderful practical judgments and penchant for detail.

All I can say at this point is that I love them both very much, and there is no doubt in my mind as to the genuineness of our venture. Amy and Karen appear to make wonderful feminine companions, so very much alike are they in disposition, character, and manner. Yet, what a splendid physical contrast they make! They love one another as well, though they are still somewhat timid physically, at least in my presence, in spite of a few sexual encounters and a three-day car trip from the Rockies to Palo Alto, during which time they became more deeply acquainted.

The interpersonal atmosphere is by no means as erotically charged as one might suspect. I anticipate highs and lows on that score. Group love just can't be that easy to come by. But there are, I am sure, silent expectations all around. Amy and I have engaged in group sex in a variety of settings any number of times. Though there were threats and stresses along the way, we are rather comfortable—depending on mood, persons present, and circumstance—in such situations, and we have observed and participated in sex with others with good results and warm feelings. Orgies are not our thing, but group sex can have a place in a full sexual life.

Wednesday, July 15 I find that I cannot easily allow myself the luxury of jealousy where Amy and Karen are concerned. Amy and I have had eight and one-half years in which we have learned about sharing one another with other persons in a comfortable way. Even when we are not so comfortable doing so—and we have by no means always been so—we are able to level with each other. We are secure in our love, and we trust very deeply.

This week Karen is spending most of her time, including nights, with a previous acquaintance who is now a lover. Before she arrived, I encouraged the relationship and urged her to sleep with him. I can't honestly say that I wish she hadn't, for in truth the man has been a wonderful influence on her. He has given her support and comfort that she much needed and has made her easier for me to love. He, too, had once experienced the joys and traumas of life with two women, during post–World War II days in Europe. He is, from her accounts, mature, sensitive, and in love with her. He is also married, a corporate executive, and some fifteen years our senior. What is more, he has charm and money and spends it quite freely.

I suppose that, being a student, it is the latter point that makes me as uncomfortable as anything else. Wealth makes me uncomfortable, and I feel that commerce and the search, the constant and unrelenting search for profit and personal gain that characterizes contemporary American life and society, taints friendship and love. However, I truly feel that such pampering is wholesome for Karen—given where she is emotionally these days—as long as she guards against substitute gratifications. And who knows what they are for anyone but oneself. I should like to be able to feel completely comfortable about the matter, and will likely succeed in doing so. In the meantime, I am somewhat perplexed, not to say annoyed with myself.

The heart of the issue is that I do not yet trust enough. I am unsure of Karen. The problem is that love can be expressed at any moment, but devotion can unfold only in time. Karen says that the other men and women in her life are but side roads and that we are the main highway. That seems true enough, for it is indeed the three of us who are going somewhere. In a mere ten days, we have become very much emotionally, physically, and intellectually involved with one another. Already we have a nascent identity as a three-person group. Our belongings, our interests, our tastes, our personalities are mingling together.

There is one point I wish to note here, since I think it will prove a problem in the future, and that is the low self-esteem with which both Karen and Amy are afflicted. I was disturbed by the fact that Amy was intimidated by Karen's physical beauty, especially last night, when, looking very delectable, Karen departed for the evening. The funny thing is that both feel the other is prettier, sexier, and so on. The truth is that they are both beautiful—almost elegant, I would say—young women in their prime. They were both pretty girls, but they are now becoming beautiful women. Amy is angular and slim and small breasted; Karen is rounded and soft and fairly large breasted. Amy admires Karen's breasts; Karen admires Amy's legs. Each feels the other is a little better off. The comparisons are not, I think, invidious, but they show in little ways how each of them is insecure.

I want very much for Karen to return to school as soon as it is financially possible. She says she wants to learn and would like to share in the intellectual pursuits that Amy and I have undertaken. Amy and I seem to be making a good team; Karen might make an excellent third. I have enough ideas for education and research to keep us all busy for a long time.

Karen has said that under different circumstances, she would have married me if I had asked. I am now speculating on the possibilities of challenging the bigamy statutes in California in order to both cement my relationship with Karen and legitimize a new way of family life. Corporate and communal families *are* realities for the future, if not the present. While it is true that our experiment is not unique, or even novel, we could take steps so that others who wished to could also participate in these new and expanded familial and sexual styles without the reservations and uncertainties we now have and will likely experience. I am amused that there are those who would label us immoral and irresponsible. So overresponsible and oversensitive are each of us at this point that we seem to confound ourselves now and then.

At the same time, there are clear advantages in being a quiet crusader merely pursuing my own private ends. All genuine social change must begin and end in the changed consciousness of the individual. To challenge a law, whether directly or indirectly, requires a genuine commitment and—exotic revolutionaries to the contrary notwithstanding—substantial resources. Besides, even though there is a clear need to update laws pertaining to family relations and sexual deviance, it is not clear that the kinds of persons who might undertake experiments like ours are in need of new laws so much as of new education, courage, and a determination to explore their own psychic and social resources. The laws need changing, to be sure, but to do so adequately will require an entirely different view of the marital relationship and its place and meaning in individual and social life. Appropriate laws can only arise from a social fabric ready to exercise them.

In addition, I do not believe that Amy or Karen could handle the conflict that would likely ensue. And if we fail as a group, we would appear pretty silly challenging bigamy statutes and arguing for new definitions of marriage and family relations when we stand as an instance of failure to transcend the old ones.

AMY

Wednesday, July 15 Jason arrived last night. Karen, nervous with anticipation, prepared for him. She looked so beautiful when she left to meet his plane: black leather boots, black velvet skirt, white blouse, and a wine-colored sweater cape trimmed with black, carrying her overnight bag and a handful of fresh daisies from us for their room. She only took enough for overnight, wanting to come back home today while he was working. Rich tried all afternoon not only not to display jealous feelings but not to have them. He asked me if I thought there was any *reason* for him to be jealous, and I reassured him that though I could certainly understand if he did feel jealous, there was not, as I saw it, any threat or *need* to feel jealous.

I feared this morning that maybe Karen would be floating on clouds and preoccupied with thoughts of Jason when she came back this afternoon. I feel badly now for even having had the thoughts because when she came in, she didn't really look happy at all. We talked, and she was disappointed because "something had been missing" with Jason. It wasn't the same as before, and she didn't know why. We all shared our feelings of how much we are becoming attached to each other.

Jason is coming for dinner with us tonight.

RICH

Thursday, July 16 I met Karen's lover last night. We all had a pleasant dinner and a comfortable evening, though the atmosphere was a bit restrained.

I found that most of my jealous feelings were dissipated by the meeting. He was a sensitive person, sad to lose Karen as a secretary and immediate friend, but certainly not a threat to me.

I had incredibly good lovemaking with Karen in the afternoon and Amy late in the evening, in spite of fatigue from too much work. I am feeling and functioning better in every way.

When it came time for them to leave last night, I had the feeling that Karen was either ambivalent or somewhat regretted her decision to spend the night with her lover. I found myself a bit shy at the door. Perhaps I am a fool to even allow either of these women to be in another man's arms, but I do not control them, and I highly value personal freedom for each of us. Besides, only the fool is secure.

It is little wonder the man fell in love with Karen. She was so emotionally abused and lonesome that she compensated by being the perfect secretary for him. In my estimation, she indulged in substitute gratification by spending much of what she earned on clothes to make herself attractive to a man who ignored her, but with whom she thought she had a life. She lived with one man in misery and worked for another for the attention she received from him. Not an unusual situation, but it has left its mark on her. Just why she continued to live with Brian, with whom she shared an apartment, is a mystery. I know she loved him and says that she just couldn't "throw in the towel" before she was sure, but I feel certain it goes much deeper and the explanation lies in her personality. In any case, I cannot see that any of the men in Karen's previous life are a threat to me, with the possible (psychoanalytic) exception of her father, with whom she had a very poor, almost nonexistent, relationship.

The two girls are so much alike in taste and manner that it is truly uncanny. When I find myself perplexed or have difficulty projecting a reaction or emotion in Karen, I substitute what I assume Amy would do. It seems to be an excellent rule of thumb so far. No doubt subtle differences will emerge in time and will make each of them more interesting in their own way. It requires extra effort to relate intimately with two persons simultaneously. Karen feels at a disadvantage at times, since Amy and I are more comfortable, even as we now alter our relationship to include a third person. We are more entrenched; we *know* each other and can respond more quickly, efficiently, and appropriately.

I must take care and make some effort to compensate for this seeming disadvantage to Karen, at the same time avoiding any unnecessary or frivolous changes with Amy. However, I feel certain that while the inclusion of a third person does change the relationship of a prior dyad, it by no means necessarily destroys or even threatens it. It depends on the level of communication and trust between those persons and the degree to which they can allow each other to grow on their own terms.

AMY

Thursday, July 16 When the three of us talked this morning, Karen said she is finding the relationship with Jason to be shallow by comparison with our threesome. He played a very important role for her before she came, but her needs and desires have changed and with them her values and their relationship. She is sleeping now, her head splitting from handling him and us at once and the conflict and pressure, as well as from wine and lack of sleep.

The first night Karen was with Jason, Rich and I slept alone. I told him I loved him and had the urge to say, "Pass it on!", as we have made a little joke of doing as three, but there was no one there to pass it on to. Strange how quickly we are three and not two or even two and one. I remember waking the morning after Karen had met (and disliked) our friends Abe and Maggie and finding her already up and out of the house. The thought welled up in my mind, "What if she's gone?", knowing that of course she wasn't, but the *void* I felt at the thought overwhelmed me. I realized I would feel lonely for her and very much miss her presence. It seems already as though she must have always been here with us.

I find I really like doing things for her, as I do for Rich, and waiting on her when I have the chance. It's fun to surprise her with little thoughtfulnesses. In fixing things in the kitchen or doing things for her, I haven't felt any resentment at all over having to fix or do for a third person or any feelings of dissatisfaction over work division, which we haven't gotten around to talking about yet. It just doesn't seem to be a big concern. That ought to stand us in good stead against building up petty grudges.

Karen has decided to stay home tonight with us rather than be with Jason again. It *is* home.

Monday, July 20 Something was bothering Karen this morning. She came out and sat down in the living room and leafed through the new *Playboy,* making no conversation and looking like something was on her mind which depressed her. This was before breakfast. I lay wrapped in the comforter in the black chair across from her. When Rich left the room, I kept still, waiting to see if and what she might say. A few times, I broke the silence with unimportant remarks intended as nondirective conversational openers to give her a chance, but they fell back after one-sentence acknowledgments.

I wait and watch. She is very quiet today. She is puttering around, putting things in place in her room. We have many little moving and organizing jobs to distract us from the project of growing together and getting to know each other better. I have to admit they distract me, too. They need to be done—both Karen and I take pleasure in having things very much in order and are a bit compulsive about that sort of thing—but they're also psychologically simple and *safe.*

Rich and I talked last night after Karen had gone to bed. We made love and ran into some conflicts and ended up talking for quite a long while. He pointed out that I had let the little things absorb me too much and that Karen and I weren't as close as we thought we were. I had to admit he was right. Karen and I are close, and there's the promise we both see of a really fantastic closeness, but we haven't moved much closer since our delightful beginning on the trip. We touch and hold and support and laugh, but we don't confront each other. We both defer to Rich on that. I should be stronger and quit putting all the responsibility on him. Otherwise, what else should I expect but that she would turn to him, as she has tended to a bit in the last few days. He pulls her out, like he always has with me, and they grow closer while she and I are lagging in our relationship. It's my own failure, produced by my insecurities, which leaves me feeling left out or secondary to him in her eyes. Insecurity breeds insecurity. And insecurities are selfish because they focus your attention on yourself and your defenses. You miss a lot that goes on around you that way.

I don't want to be secondary in her eyes, just like I don't want her to be secondary in Rich's eyes. The three of us as a family won't really work that way. Each of us would have needs that weren't being met; Karen especially would feel the need for the love of a man for whom she was primary. Only if that desire is fulfilled will she be happy with us for any period of time. We have room for her in the middle, at the "center," as she called it when she asked Rich the other day if there was room there for her. We want her to participate in the real heart of our feelings, to feel her as deeply as we feel each other. But does she have room for me at the center?

Karen came out to the kitchen a bit ago, and I snagged her on her way back out and asked what was bothering her, looking at her in a way to let her know I could read her. She rambled about a budding headache; she gets them badly, but they seem to have some connection with psychological stress in her. When she finished, I said, "I can see you hiding in there" (meaning inside herself). She responded that she just felt like being quiet and by herself today. True enough, but I'm sure there's something behind her feeling that way; I don't think she is feeling a positive and healthy desire for solitude like everyone needs some of the time. Maybe I'm wrong, because she really hasn't had much time to herself since she got here, and I thoroughly respect that need as I defend it for myself. But that's not all there is to it this time. She feels insecure today, but I don't know why. Is it us or Jason's departure or something else? I hope she will share her feelings with us tonight and ease our ignorance and concern. Rich can see something is bothering her, too.

Karen hasn't started writing in her journal yet. I know that disappoints Rich, but he hasn't said anything to her. He doesn't want to pressure her, but I know it bothers him.

Karen has been awfully busy with Jason here, as she said this morning when we were talking briefly about the journals in another context. But I suppose we could all always be too busy or not ever find the time to write in them. So it raises the question of priorities, and that's what bothers Rich. My first reaction, characteristically, is to feel threatened, to feel maybe she's not as serious about the three-way relationship as we are, though it could just be the journal idea she's not serious about. Maybe there's no problem there either. I think I'm oversensitive, since Karen and I have not been growing closer. I miss that and have got to put some constructive thought and effort into it.

My God, it's complicated with three! No one's mood is independent of the others'.

KAREN

Tuesday, July 21 It's about time I stop putting off writing in my journal and start placing on paper the thoughts and feelings inside me beginning July 4. I'm afraid I won't be able to adequately record the changes in my life, then *or* now. July 4, 1970, began a whole new life for me; it is comforting and warm but at the same time breathtaking and scary. Every day is new and exciting, and anything less would be narrow and boring.

Actually, this whole thing started long before our current efforts at a group marriage. I met Rich in Los Angeles five years ago, and we dated there. Rich was living with Amy at the time, and I remember being at a loss for words when he told me he did indeed have a girl friend and, yes, she was in Los Angeles also. My feelings for Rich grew, and I fell in love with him knowing he would be marrying Amy. We met again (prearranged) in San Francisco, by which time Rich and Amy were married, and I was (to all intents and purposes) living with Brian. My feelings for Rich never changed; they may have been shuffled around a bit, but they were nevertheless just as strong. Brian decided to go to school in Dallas, and I followed about six weeks later. During those six weeks after Brian had left, I saw Rich. We made love; we laughed and talked; I loved him still, married and all. On the day I was to leave—a brisk and foggy San Francisco morning, as I recall—he drove up to San Francisco, helped me pack the car, gave me the goodie bag Amy had prepared, and saw me off. He didn't want me to leave, I knew that, but he encouraged me to make my own decision based on my own wants and needs. For the next several years, we corresponded. As time went on, there were phone calls and finally tapes. Our feelings deepened and grew. My life in Dallas was miserable, and after about a year and a half, I called Rich. I was in tears, and I was so miserable. I suppose that was the seed. Rich and Amy sent me a check and said, "Don't be unhappy; we'll help." I felt I couldn't accept; perhaps I hadn't tried hard enough. I went through another two years of unhappiness, but when I split with Brian, I was *sure* it couldn't work for us. When, one Sunday, Rich called and said, "Would you like to come live with us?", I answered unhesitatingly, "Yes."

It was decided that on my way back to San Francisco, I would swing up through the Rockies where Rich and Amy were visiting his parents, spend a few days there, and then while Rich flew home, Amy and I would drive back. This would give us time to get to know one another.

As I was driving toward our rendezvous, my mind was working faster and faster. I had committed myself to people whom I hadn't seen for three and a half years, to a girl I barely know—jeez! When I turned off the main road, I saw a big Welcome Karen sign strung across the road, and Rich and Amy came out as I pulled to a stop by the house. My very first thoughts were, "Rich's hair is longer than I've ever seen it," and "Amy is prettier and tinier than I remembered."

I arrived on Saturday, July 4, and we left for Denver on Monday to drive Rich to the airport and to begin our drive to San Francisco. Perhaps because I was tired, or maybe the time simply wasn't appropriate, we didn't make love during the initial stay with Rich's parents. I was glad; I needed time to stabilize myself.

For two days, Amy and I were sort of checking each other out. We were quiet and just at loose ends when Rich wasn't around. We spent most of the two days just talking and getting to feel at ease with each other.

Amy and I were—and are, but to a much lesser degree— shy with each other. The cross-country drive put us together in a way that nothing else I can think of would have.

When we saw Rich off at the airport, we got our first taste of outside reaction to the three of us. Amy and I both were aware of mildly curious glances at the boyishly good-looking man with an attractive young woman on each arm. The mildly curious glances changed into puzzled stares as Rich lovingly kissed us both as he walked to his departure gate. Chapter One of our outside exposure!

The question of bisexuality has been the topic of many discussions. I really didn't know quite what to expect. I had always thought Amy to be sexy, but, well, suppose we just simply didn't hit it off? That, of course, wasn't the case. We *did* hit it off, and I became increasingly curious about my feelings for her and hers for me. I don't think either of us actually thought we would make love on our way across country, though there was much good-natured kidding about it. We had revealed (with some prodding from Rich) that each of us had had a previous sexual experience with another girl. But that in itself is another story.

Our drive-time talking ran the gamut from our sexual experiences to family life to favorite foods. We became acquainted in a concentrated fashion.

When we stopped at the end of the first day of driving, and after dinner, showers, etcetera, we *did* make love. (I made love to Amy but didn't encourage her to make love to me. Explore why!) It came naturally, though we were both shy. I felt clumsy, not knowing how far to go or if I might offend. Our lovemaking was sweet, and I suppose I would describe it as innocent rather than hungrily passionate.

We didn't make love again on the trip. The feelings were there, but our shyness and fears of offending the other kept our advances on the affection level.

We made excellent time, and upon our arrival in Reno, we called Rich and told him we'd be home about noon of the following day. He asked us to delay it a few hours so everything would be ready for us. We spent the next morning driving around the Lake Tahoe–Squaw Valley area and picnicking by a stream and then headed for San Francisco and our final destination, Palo Alto, arranging to arrive about 5:00 P.M.

When we pulled up, Rich was standing at the picture window. We were home. *Finally,* after all the letters, phone calls, tapes, discussions, here we were—beginning a new life as a threesome.

Rich had the house clean, and there were surprises for both Amy and me. Dinner was ready, and shortly after our arrival, two dozen roses were delivered: a dozen long-stemmed yellow roses for Amy and a dozen long-stemmed red roses for me. What a delightful homecoming!

After a relaxing dinner and relating all our experiences to Rich, Amy left Rich and me to make love alone—our first time in over three years. The lovemaking was superb, and my orgasm was accompanied by a flood of tears—relief, happiness, excitement, and release of emotions and feelings.

Amy and I had arrived on Thursday, July 9. On Tuesday, July 14, Jason arrived. Jason is my former boss and present lover. Without his support and understanding and reinforcement—Well, when I needed someone, he was there.

It was unfortunate that he arrived here on business so soon

after our arrival home. It was unhealthy for my relationship with Rich and Amy, which was so new and tender. But we made the best of it, and after discussing our feelings about it many times, I had no choice but to leave my new home. I drove to the airport to meet Jason with mixed feelings.

I spent the week Jason was here shuffling back and forth between his hotel and home. He came to dinner on Wednesday evening and liked Amy immediately, but I could sense a reluctance to accept Rich. I felt Rich was somewhat uncomfortable, but Amy compensated beautifully. Dinner was pleasant, and Jason entertained us. We made plans to go to the beach together on the following Sunday.

The day couldn't have been more beautiful. We had a great time, but Rich was tired and somewhat quiet, and of course Jason interpreted this as a slight to him. *I* felt he was looking for things to interpret negatively.

While Jason was here, he went to see a personal friend of his who also happens to be a psychiatrist. After relating the story of my relationship with him and with Rich and Amy, the psychiatrist told him in essence I had sought the relationship with Rich and Amy because I didn't know how to love. Boy, that scared the hell out of me. Jason had said virtually the same thing before. He related all this to me while we were at the beach on Sunday. I tried to keep it inside, like I always had done, and work it out myself, but it really upset me. Amy could tell something was bothering me yesterday, and so could Rich. I finally broke down and told them what Jason had said and how it frightened me. Sharing the bad is harder for me than sharing the good.

RICH

Wednesday, July 22 On Saturday last, we took Karen to a nude party, a ho-hum affair that was crowded and noisy. She had been curious about them, wanting to test her own interests by attending such a gathering. I knew she was nervous during the afternoon, but I had no idea how insecure and shy she really is about such things. She spent the evening in a "safe" basket chair, terribly defensive and critical of the others there. It's true there were many phonies there; we were all aware of that. But she made no effort to reach out or communicate, did not dance, swim, or remove her clothes, though when we took her to such a party several years ago, she had thoroughly enjoyed herself. It may have simply been a function of mood, but I think not; rather, it was a consequence of personality structure.

As she prepared for the evening, she seemed to literally paint on her confidence in the form of cosmetics. And whatever else may be true of swinging parties, it *is* true that clothes and makeup mask the person. I encountered her without makeup; she was very sensitive about it. She feels she is not pretty, is too fat, etcetera. At the same time, she disclosed curiosity about seeing men nude, about watching couples engaged in coitus, about group sex, and so on. In a word, she is repressed, and her low self-esteem manifested itself under pressure.

Sunday we spent the day driving to a beach and having a picnic. It was a nice, relaxed afternoon. In the evening, we were all tired, but Amy and I talked and made love till 3:00 A.M. Amy agreed that she and Karen were having some problems getting in touch with each other despite the three-day car trip and the intimacy they shared then. They have a bad set of priorities, wanting to work on the house first and each other's personalities second. They are hardly aware of this, or if so, they hide it. I will have to be both strong and clever without being overbearing—a difficult task for me.

I am uncomfortable when they hide, when they cannot come out, when they cannot disclose. I guess the truth is that when they hide, I am lonely, and I fear being lonely. Now that Amy is more aware of the problem, she may be able to provoke Karen into an interpersonal confrontation. Amy now knows the value of it but says she does not know how. If nothing else, I shall remedy it by a few days in the camper. Long walks in the daytime and long talks at night should help. We *must* learn to be as candid in our three-person group as we each are in various two-person arrangements. The difficulty is that Karen's two-person situations were something less than satisfactory, and she has learned to wear masks without detection; sometimes without even self-detection.

Our friends Kathy and Bob say they are about to expand their marriage also. I think we have inspired and encouraged them. I wish them well if they are serious about it. But I feel that while it is good to conceive expanding one's emotional life, it can't be done by seeking a person to fill a slot. On the other hand, some individuals do decide to get married and then proceed to seek out a mate. In the absence of comparative results of such strategies, who can say with certainty which will lead to success and happiness? I really wish they weren't leaving the area. They are such good companions, and Karen took to them immediately. Such friends will be difficult to replace.

KAREN

Wednesday, July 22 Last Saturday, we were invited to a nude party at Whit and Sandy's, friends of Rich and Amy. What a disaster! It was my period; I felt fat and ugly. I was uncomfortable and defensive. So I retreated to a corner of the room, sat in a big rattan hanging chair, turned my back to the party, and dozed off, hoping I would awaken to find the party had been only a nightmare. I kept thinking, "What the hell am I doing here? What's the point of it all?"

Part of the problem was that we also took Joyce. She is the girl Amy first made love with, and I disliked her immediately. Amy had written me about her while I was still in

Texas. When I got the letter in which she said she had had a relationship with a gal—Well, I was at work, and fortunately, no one was in the office except Luann, the other secretary. I read the letter, and my face must have fallen at least two miles. I couldn't help it, and the tears started. I remember it scared the hell out of Luann; she didn't know what had happened, thinking perhaps one of my parents was ill or had died. Anyway, it really shook me. I had so looked forward to being the first. Why, I wonder? I mean it really doesn't matter, or does it? Anyway, my own first homosexual experience—with Luann—was triggered by that letter. I said, "What the hell—" Until then, I had been saving myself for Amy.

On the way to the party, Amy and I sat in the back seat; and Amy, sensing my insecurity, kept squeezing my hand and reassuring me. I was glad when the evening was over. In defiance, I hadn't undressed. It probably didn't prove anything to anyone else, but it was my way of—of what? Protesting, perhaps?

I've had some difficulty adjusting to no routine, no time schedule; I couldn't seem to get anything accomplished. I kept meaning to start this journal, but the longer I put it off, the more I became afraid of writing. At the same time, I began to feel more and more comfortable in our home. I felt so awkward in the kitchen at first. However, as I was quickly discovering, Amy and I are so similar; we are so alike, it's really scary sometimes.

I have been busy unpacking all my boxes sent from Dallas and rediscovering things I'd forgotten about which had been in storage for three and a half years. Toward the end of my unpacking and sorting, I came to the realization that I had been trying to bribe Amy—Rich, too, for that matter—with my possessions. They would like me if I had pretty things to share with them. Wow! That really shook me up, and I did some reexamining.

I have an unfortunate feeling; Rich calls it "low self-esteem." And what is even worse, Amy suffers from it, too. It isn't difficult for me to find all the things that are wrong with me; they seem so numerous and so obvious. What I need to display is more of a sense of self and self-love. That being difficult for me is undoubtedly a reason for my being attracted to and admiring people who display self-confidence.

Our first lovemaking as a threesome was such a unique experience for me; I can't begin to describe the warmth, closeness, and depth of feeling. I felt like a bride. It was so new; I had never experienced anything like it. I felt somewhat shy making individual overtures toward Amy and/or toward Rich, shy at knowing someone was watching, was present, but that was one of the easiest hang-ups to rid myself of. All the inhibitions are so cumbersome and uncomfortable. It feels so good to drop them; sort of like the relief you'd feel taking off a heavy, fur-lined topcoat in ninety-degree weather.

One fear which made me uncomfortable, and still does a bit, is regarding my lovemaking with Amy. *I'm* afraid *she* won't be able to satisfy *me*—and not because she won't try or know how or whatever, but that *I* won't be able to let go and enjoy just being pleased. So I've kind of subconsciously been keeping her advances confined to affection; I don't encourage much sexual play or flirt with her or make advances. I'm so afraid she'd be hurt if I weren't orgasmic. I think I'm a bit stronger and would be able to bounce back more easily if the situation were reversed. I could be mistaken. I also feel somewhat reserved about making love to her in front of Rich. For some reason, I'd prefer it more private, at least until I become more—more what? Skilled? Comfortable? Uninhibited?

I'm more tender and easily hurt and more jealous of Amy than I am of Rich. I'm extremely hostile toward Joyce. Why? Perhaps because she was "the first" for Amy, perhaps because of the impact Amy's telling me via letter had, perhaps

GARDNER WEBB COLLEGE LIBRARY

because I don't care for her personally. Or maybe I'm hiding, maybe because I think she's prettier or sexier or can please Amy better!

The first time she came over, I was quite defensive and hostile. Rich had gone to bed. The three of us were talking, and I walked out to the kitchen to get something to drink, and I became aware of what I was doing. *They* wanted to be alone, and *I* was guarding Amy! What a shock! I really couldn't believe what I was doing. I felt so very, very foolish and wanted to go to my room, but Amy and Joyce were in the living room, which I would have to go through. I kept thinking what I should do and finally decided, "I live here; I'll just walk right through to my room." I did. Amy and Joyce were embracing, and I remember the awful sinking feeling inside.

I remember preparing for bed and trying to talk myself out of the bad feelings I had. Apparently I didn't talk fast enough because the tears came and the ugly feelings and the frustration. When Joyce left, Amy came in my room to see if I was OK, and I said I was "thinking of Jason" and was just "feeling sad." I don't seem much good at concealing my feelings anymore. I was once, but as you open up more, as you reveal more of yourself and let others inside and love and care for them, it becomes almost impossible to hide. A rough lesson and a painful one for me to learn.

The first friends of Rich and Amy I met were Abe and Maggie. Hoo-boy! Immediate dislike. I couldn't decide who I disliked more—Maggie because of her prowling around Rich, or Abe because of the way he touched Amy. I still can't resolve my feelings about them. I know them better now, and I guess I'd describe my feeling in this way: "They're OK, I guess." Perhaps that's *some* progress. As people go, they're OK, but I'd resent it if Rich went to bed with Maggie because I'd view it as servicing her. That's always the impression I get of her; she's on the prowl for someone to service her.

RICH

Thursday, July 23 What a wonderful time we are having! Karen's lover left a few days ago, so her attentions are no longer divided. She is the one most relieved.

He did an unfortunate thing, perhaps intentionally, perhaps not. He went to a psychiatrist friend in San Francisco, told him what he knew of the three of us, and told Karen that the good doctor said the reason she was entering into a relationship with Amy and me was that she did not know how to love. It's true that Karen has difficulty expressing certain feelings, but I interpret this as the result of a miserable family situation and of indifference and selfishness on the part of Brian, the guy she lived with and tried to love for three years. It was *he* who did not appreciate her many attempts to please him. During their last year, they made love only infrequently because he was too busy, too unconcerned, too selfish. This caused Karen to close up and wither emotionally.

In consulting the psychiatrist, Jason may have been himself seeking some authority to confirm his own opinions, a common phenomenon in our society, where psychiatrists become sometimes reluctant but always compelling moralists. He may only have been saying that Karen was not loving *him* the way *he* wished. An all-too-smug psychiatrist once told me that my plan to live with Amy and Karen was mere wish fulfillment. When I told him about the idea, he replied, "That's a pleasant fantasy. What do you make of it?" I'm sure he thought I was putting him on.

The whole thing hurt Karen, and she was fearful of disclosing it to us. She was confused and upset but finally let it all out. I say she is a loving woman, very much so, so much so that she has a need to be needed that has gone unfulfilled for some time. It can now be fulfilled if she likes; all (all!) she has to do is trust. This is complicated by the fact that Amy and I are an ongoing group and know each other well.

Karen cannot hide her upsets very well, any more than

Amy can. I have a dozen little cues already: eye contact, nervousness, shyness amid affection, and so on. I must learn these things thoroughly with Karen, though the pressure to do so makes it somewhat more difficult. A failure in such interpersonal sensitivity could cost us dearly. One odd point, which is both an advantage and a disadvantage, depending on how and to what degree one accepts and integrates it, is that there is always a third to monitor those feelings. In a competitive environment, this leads to undesirable consequences, since the one doing the monitoring can exploit the monitored person's errors rather than simply be the brunt of them. But if the third person has a stake in the positive relationship between the other two—that is, if the relationship is a potentially rewarding or synergistic one—he or she can seek to improve that relationship by providing sympathetic but usefully critical feedback to the other two. If the positive elements are present, it should be *easier* for two persons to become acquainted and more intimate in the presence of and through the help of a third. In a certain sense, a threesome is like having a built-in marriage counselor from the beginning.

We are like persons on a honeymoon, and indeed that is what I planned for the summer. Amy and Karen are having more trouble letting go of routine than I am. Amy flurries about tending house and meals, while Karen unpacks box after box.

Our sexual interaction is improving. Amy and Karen enjoy making love together, and they admire each other's bodies. Two nights ago, we made love for a long time and were more comfortable and satisfied together than ever before. Yesterday afternoon, Amy came in while Karen and I were fucking and joined us for an hour or more. It was a wonderful, lazy afternoon. We are like children together, exploring, feeling, caressing, learning the secrets of group love and three way sex. They please me a great deal, and I am enough of

a voyeur to get warm pleasure watching them in their feminine embraces.

They are very gentle with one another and thus provide a
good lesson for me. It makes me think, albeit onesidely, that
much of the inclination to lesbian love is a matter of compensation for the gruff forcefulness and lack of languorous and
extended foreplay of the male. What the male fails to perceive is that not only is the capacity for repeated orgasmic
response greater than his own (a fact that no doubt intimi-
dates many men) but also that a woman's erogenous areas
are broader, more diffuse. More of her skin surface and nerve
bundles are capable of erotic stimulation and involvement.
Her response is more varied, more complex, and therefore
more absorbing, more complete. While the sexual specialists
argue to and fro about clitoral versus vaginal orgasms,
healthy women who are really alive and uninhibited continue
to experience orgasmic responses with and through their
entire bodies. They become virtually electric to the touch,
their hair stands on end, and their entire bodies writhe and
contort in search of a total release of sexual tension.

Last night, we all had dinner at Kathy and Bob's and
wound up in a glorious sexual pile at 3:00 A.M. Everyone
enjoyed it. Karen felt quite at ease, even though it was her
first such experience with a group of that sort. Kathy and
Bob are close friends, sensitive, intelligent, attractive people.
Karen found them delightful company, and Bob was a good
lover to her. Because I trust Bob and Kathy so much, I found
myself feeling as comfortable about Karen being with him as
I do about Amy, and that is a relief. Kathy and I had not
made love for some time, and I had missed her. I feel love
for her as well, and we shall all miss them when they leave
for their new jobs in New England.

If I have had any worries about the lingering potency
effects of fatigue caused by the virus attacks, they were dispelled by seven orgasms yesterday. We all had a good laugh

when I remarked about it. I felt like an overactive teen-ager
with a constant erection, though I was thoroughly sated by
the end of the day.

Friday, July 24 I think that it would not be irrelevant here
to include some comments concerning my own sexual history as well as a few details concerning my attitudes toward
women, inasmuch as I think they account for some of my
own behavior leading to a companionate family experiment
for myself. I believe that my sexual history for the most part
has been what might be called *supernormal.* That is to say,
in my estimation, it has been healthy in almost every respect.

To begin with, it is pertinent to note that I am a highly
sexed individual. This is a part of my physiological makeup.
I was, until my severe skiing accident two years ago, an
extremely healthy person; I am still very active, energetic,
outgoing. My own inward attitude toward my sexuality may
be summed up by saying that I attempt to repress my sexual
feelings and desires as little as possible. My sexual feelings
toward the outside world are extremely liberal—nay, radical
—and may be summed up by saying: Live and let live. I
believe sexual repression to be one of the greatest evils which
has ever befallen mankind and ranks on a par with war,
poverty, and racism as a social issue.

It might be of interest to note that one of my earliest
childhood sexual experiences was a threesome, at the age of
nine or ten, in a tree house. Two curious lads escorted a
prepubescent girl-next-door to their aerie, provoked her to
undress, and then pondered what to do next. As for group
sex, covert though it may be, what teen-ager has not been
aroused by the activities of the couple in the back seat or the
next room? I was no exception. Neither was I spared the
allure of strip shows, by overweight women old enough to be
my mother, a decade or more in advance of the topless
culture.

The usual pornography came my way from a wide range
of various though usually peer sources, including, for a fact,

Gray's legendary anatomy text as a preteen all the way to hard-core stag movies at fraternity smokers as a college freshman. My first love affair, at the age of fifteen with a steady girl one year my senior, was coitally consummated, after a year of dating and petting, on a sunny April day, at home, in bed, with much playfulness and mutual satisfaction. It would be fair to say that we taught one another how to make love, for we both were nominal virgins at the time.

I had no other sexual partners until well into my sophomore year at college, except for two homosexual contacts during the summer prior to my senior year in high school. They were experimental, they did not seem threatening, and they were not particularly satisfying. I now believe that had they been satisfying, my sexual life might have been somewhat different. That is to say, I might have become bisexual at the time, as I think all truly normal and really sexually integrated people would become if they were not so effectively channeled and socialized.

I had the customary masturbation fantasies about my female teachers, movie starlets, and *Playboy* centerfolds. And though in moments of what might be called pressing need the idea appealed to me, I never joined in the midnight rush to the harlot's den. The idea of buying a woman's body in order to gain pleasure from it is anathema to me. Actually, it makes me sad that there is, and has been throughout history, so little love in the world that a woman's genitals (and men's as well, to be sure) become a commodity, a negotiable item to be consumed for a price. It's not that it is wrong or immoral, just tragically unnecessary.

At sixteen, I read, somewhat uncomprehendingly to be sure, Brill's lectures on psychoanalysis. At about the same time, I read Albert Ellis's *American Sexual Tragedy* with great interest. From that time forward, my sexual consciousness was forever changed. Society was based upon multiple forms of sexual repression, and I was an incipient rebel against the status quo. I had experienced it as any youth does. It hurt. It stunted my emotional growth. My feelings were molded by something outside me, something alien to my nature, something unnecessary for my world. For the first time, it had a name, a label: the Puritan ethic. Dimly cognizant of its effects, I was determined to be rid of it.

In the latter two years of my undergraduate life, I became sexually quite active. I can only say that women have always been good to me. There is one noteworthy exception, and that was a girl I became involved with in college who taught me the meaning of sexual jealousy, a lesson I shall never forget nor do I ever wish to repeat. It is an unnecessary and pointless emotion. It is not a normal reaction. And it is something which squanders one's resources in a rather self-defeating way.

Since my undergraduate years, I have had a good many sexual partners, sometimes in very casual ways, sometimes in a sustained and deep way. I have fond memories of almost all of them. Some of them have been truly beautiful and very sexually exciting women. I regard my sexual life as full, active, and healthy.

I have found that the women who are the best lovers are those who are the most personally mature and open. This is not to say that a woman cannot have an exciting, sensuous, desirable body and be a good sexual partner on that account alone. But this does not allow for that interpersonal rapport which adds graceful and meaningful touches to sexual interaction. Women whose sexuality is muffled and constrained tend not so much to be frigid, although I am sure there are a number who fall into that category, but simply to be dull, flat, and boring.

I find myself very much aware of women in my daily comings and goings. Some of my students are very attractive to me. I often feel like making love to my friends who are women. I enjoy their caresses, their smooth voices, and their passion and warmth. And I enjoy seeing in them what are sometimes thought of as masculine traits, although to say that they are masculine traits is an error, a projection of masculine chauvinistic notions which in fact drive a wedge between the sexes. That is, I enjoy to see in women courage, self-reliance, and a certain measure of initiative which expresses itself in healthy feminine form.

I suppose many of these attitudes stem from the fact that my parents have such a healthy, loving relationship even now into their fifties, for my mother and father worked closely together to develop a small business for twenty years, after which they retired to spend all of their time together fishing, hiking, gardening, and traveling. My parents are still very affectionate with one another, and I have every reason to think that they have always had a sexually healthy relationship, albeit an exclusive and somewhat possessive one. I had a good model.

When I married Amy, I had good reason to believe we would be happy together, but I didn't realize what an exciting interpersonal adventure it would be. Except for trips back to Colorado and Michigan to our respective families, we have been virtually constant companions since we met. We loved well; we lived harmoniously without money or jobs; we studied together; and we liked traveling together. We talked for hours on end, discovered similarities in taste and values, compatibilities in style and manner, and lived together off and on for one and a half years before marrying. Marriage was a formality, a convenience, a requisite legality to satisfy state, church, family, and the general social order. I recall that the officiating minister was irritated at our apparent lack of concern over the seriousness of the service. He is now divorced.

Amy blossomed as a student, won fellowships easily, and is now doing first-rate graduate work. The funny thing is that at one time she was very cautious about returning to school. She was unsure of herself, afraid of failure, and so on. After a lengthy talk with Karen the other night, we discovered similar fears and uncertainties. More low self-esteem. But just as with Amy, I think I have spotted real but latent intellectual potential, among other things.

I told Karen I very much wanted her to return to school and that we would help in any way we could. At this point, the most important factor seems to be simple encouragement without pressure. It would please me no end if Karen could get a degree in a collateral field and we could then expand our research efforts from two to three, along with the other aspects of our lives. We shall see. I am hopeful.

Many persons, especially the rigid professionals in psychiatry and counseling, would view our experiment as a way to buttress a sagging marriage. The truth of the matter is that I fell in love with both of them and never lied about or knowingly distorted my feelings regarding Karen or Amy at any time. Amy and I had decided on an open marriage from the start. Far brom buttressing a poor marriage, we are rather expanding a good one in order to make it better yet. At the very least, one might say that it is such adventures and experiments which, consciously and conscientiously pursued, keep a marriage always viable, always fulfilling, always growing.

Monday, July 27 Everyone is out of sorts today. I'm sure it will lift by the end of the day, but now the atmosphere is tense.

Last night, Kathy and Bob came over. I had hoped for a pleasant, relaxed evening together, perhaps with a measure of lovemaking where all participate. I knew something was awry within thirty minutes after their arrival, but I could not tell what. After about two hours, it came out: Kathy and Bob wanted to take Karen home with them for the night. In other words, as I saw it, Bob wanted to appropriate her. He put it politely enough, but somehow the whole thing was thoughtless and misconceived. Karen was flattered but ambivalent. She enjoys her new freedom but saw correctly that we are not yet stable enough to handle such matters. She declined the invitation.

The whole thing hurt Amy, perhaps deeply, and it surprised and disturbed me. We could all have stayed here and made love in any combination. Amy says that Bob is on an "ego trip." I don't know for sure, but I'm glad Karen didn't go. Karen thinks that Kathy and Bob are envious of our happiness.

We had a group embrace last night. Everyone kissed and hugged, but when I made a gesture to Bob, he shied away. It was odd. I now have a glimmer of Amy's contentions about how most persons shut out half the human species because they happen to be of the same sex. Truly absurd.

Amy and I stayed up till 3:00 A.M. talking after Bob and Kathy left and after I had made very relaxed and free and uncontrolled love to Amy and Karen. Out of fear of getting my partners pregnant and a desire to please, I learned as a teen-ager to be very controlled with my orgasms, so much so that while orgasms are not a problem, letting go (inside somewhere) is. But I feel I am relearning quickly. They are each and both very loving.

We three sleep together in a king-size bed. Much of the time I had been the meat in the middle of the sandwich. Last night, partly because she was upset, Karen and I put Amy in the middle and held her for a long time. I think she enjoyed it; she said it felt warm and cozy. It does.

KAREN

Monday, July 27 Kathy and Bob are two of Rich and Amy's closest friends. I liked them both immediately and felt no hostility or jealousy toward either of them. They invited us over for dinner one evening, and we all made love: Bob, Amy, and I and Kathy and Rich. We all felt very close and warm. That was the night of my famous last words: "Is this group sex?" Afterward, Rich and Amy asked me how I felt and whether or not I was threatened or jealous in any way. I replied that I had nothing but good feelings about the entire evening. I felt a very strong relationship growing between the five of us, but this was soon to be interrupted by Kathy and Bob leaving for the East. Shortly before we were to leave for a vacation to Los Angeles and then Baja California, Kathy and Bob came over one evening. Toward the end of that evening, they asked if I would like to go home and spend the night with them. I was *very flattered* but admit I felt somewhat put upon. I felt a bit pressured by time and circumstances. I turned them down gently, and after they left, Rich and Amy and I had a long discussion. I couldn't go; I would have been uneasy and uptight, though I care for Kathy and Bob. Rich and Amy and I weren't stable enough yet; my leaving so soon to be with Kathy was dangerous. Amy was more upset afterward than she appeared at the time. Was it because of me with Kathy and Bob, and Rich and Amy not being there? Or was it Kathy and me?

Something else: When Bob and Kathy left, we had a fivesome kiss. Not as sexy as a threesome kiss, but still nice. When we were all kissing and hugging in the circle, Rich made a gesture to Bob, and Bob shied away. It was so obvious, though Rich recovered quickly. I felt so sorry for him. Rich has mentioned several times he is curious about how deep his homosexual feelings are. I wish I could help him find someone with whom to explore and examine them.

RICH

Tuesday, July 28 I sometimes fear Karen's priorities and needs are not quite, or not quite yet, compatible with mine. She, to my knowledge, has hardly written anything in her journal yet. It is beginning to disturb me. And Amy, too, who says and does nothing. I have made suggestions, allusions, etcetera, without demanding or cajoling.

One thing that is really going to bother me is if Karen does not level with persons she meets about herself, her relationship to Amy and me, our living arrangement, and so on.

Total disclosure is neither necessary nor appropriate, but deception, especially since it will distort her relationship to me as well as Amy, I will not accept. Amy and I made up our minds to *live it out.* I confided in my parents and most of our close friends. I want Karen to be equally open with *her* friends.

We leave for Mexico day after tomorrow.

Thursday, July 30

> Face to face to face,
> Searching for warm sun and water.
> Feelings of freedom.

AMY

Friday, August 7 I'm struggling for peace, but it is hard to unwind and soothe my frayed nerves from days of driving, always on the move. Periods of solitude have been rarely interspersed with our togetherness in the camper on the road. The camping trip down into Baja California was largely a disappointment, very dry and dusty countryside devoid of the secluded sunny beaches we were in search of. We did, however, experience being dirty together in close proximity, and the bathroom barriers have been lowered as we all frequently made "shi-shi" (as Karen calls urinating, after the Japanese) at the side of the road. But we really accomplished little else the last week.

We're now in the mountains of California in a national forest, camped beside a little stream where we will stay over the weekend. At last, we are stopped and out of the car! I have had my fill of driving. As soon as we found the campsite, Karen and I each packed a lunch and separately set out in search of private nooks, each of us feeling the same need I think: the need to be alone, not to hide, not to withdraw from a problem (as admittedly we are both wont to do), just a need for some time alone.

Rich has such a hard time understanding that need, for he is always suspicious that it is grounded in withdrawal from a problem. He is the guardian of our neurotic withdrawal behavior, our avoidance responses, ever alert and shouldering the stress of that position by choice because of his fervent commitment to communication. How I appreciate him for that! I think most of the time he knows that I do even when I struggle against him. I have come to struggle less when he catches me withdrawing because I have come to understand better now what he is striving for, and I desire the same and am more able to handle the challenge of openness, the opening up of myself to myself and to others. But he must come to appreciate, value, and guard the healthy need to be alone, the embracing of internal peace and consolidation which is then brought back and shared, and the sheer need for occasional periods of just plain solitude and solitary pursuits which in turn increase the awareness of the opposite pleasures of togetherness.

As we each withdraw less and hide from problems less when they are felt and present, he will feel less need to guard us all against that. But in the meantime, he must become an even more sensitive discerner of which of our needs for solitude is in ascendance, the healthy or the unhealthy. Otherwise he will burden us all with a tension, a heaviness that will harm our togetherness and be counterproductive to our growth, for we will have to strain against it and mix our pleasures of being together with resentment over unmet needs to be alone. When needs are unsatisfied, they grow out of proportion, and this one blown up could only be destructive of our whole attempt. I wish he would realize this.

I have sat here and tried to examine myself openly and cannot find any problem that my need to be alone for a while stems from. I have recognized in myself for some time a need to feel off duty. Rich and I have discussed that, as I had a heightened awareness of it while caring for him this last year while he struggled with the aftermath of his accident. I need to have times when I am not on call or trying to anticipate and respond to another's needs, times when there are no meals or drinks or snacks to fix. This is alleviated by Karen's presence. By sharing these things, we each gain time. There is an alternate to fill Rich's needs and demands and our own, for we both seem to delight in doing things for each other, as Rich does in doing things for each of us. Karen is less used to attending to another over long periods of time than I, so I suspect part of her need to be alone today is also based on off-duty time. For her, the new challenge of authentic searching and showing of self is more demanding, and she needs rest periods from that, too.

The only problem—and it is a problem—that hangs over me with the three of us is my need and desire *to be desired* by Karen sexually. This remains unresolved, and I am insecure and awkward about it. I want her to turn to me; I want her to really desire to make love with me; I want to touch her and feel her become sincerely aroused and know that it is I who am arousing her and giving her pleasure. If I can arouse her, I can learn to satisfy her; but I cannot satisfy her if I cannot arouse her. Until then, I will have flare-ups of jealousy when others do what I have not yet been able to share with her. Jealousy *has* a basis when there is a deficit or a loss or something shared with another which is not shared with you. When you have something, then jealousy can be purged from the sharing of the same with another, for it is something you already have and are not losing by the other having it, too. For example, when Rich observes little courtesies with Karen or restrains an impatient response because it is Karen who is helping him with a frustrating task (like loading the luggage rack on top of the car!) or flirts with Karen in ways one does with someone new, I feel some jealousy. I know it is only because he and I know each other so well and have such easy and satisfying familiarity that he is different with me. Perhaps Karen feels some jealousy over our familiarity when it is evidenced, but I still feel jealous because they share something then that I would like, even though he and I share something very special that I also like.

This same problem occurs in terms of demands, and the three of us have discussed it a little. Rich is not comfortable yet in making demands on Karen, though he is progressing. Things like asking Karen to get something for him or to iron a pair of slacks he wants to wear. It also shows up sexually somewhat in that I feel a responsibility to satisfy him sexually, even if just by hand, before he goes to sleep; otherwise, I know he will have a difficult time falling asleep. I would resent it if I was not in the mood for sex or was too tired and so was Karen and if he were then *always* to turn to me. He has been just *great* about not doing that, though, poor dear, I know it must be fantastically hard for him on occasion to be unsatisfied between two desirable but undesiring women! That's been harder for him in the camper than at home because we have both been tired and dirty from driving and less interested in sex at bedtime and also because there's no place else to go to seek privacy to masturbate. We haven't yet overcome the masturbation barrier, though we all acknowledge that we masturbate. We will desensitize ourselves on that soon by the three of us masturbating side by side. That ought to do it! I remember that was embarrassing for Rich and me to overcome together, and that technique worked with us. So does masturbating with another augmenting and helping. We'll get to that before long.

I feel at peace now. It has been cathartic to focus on my feelings alone and commit them to paper, and I have now had a period of solitude. I don't know how long I've been sitting here close to the water in a hidden nook. I'm more able to appreciate the gurgling and bubbling of the stream over the rocks at my feet, and I am ready to go back soon and join Rich and Karen if she has returned refreshed as I. How I love them both! I hope Rich has not been lonely or unhappy while we've been gone.

RICH

Friday, August 7 Mexico was hot, dry, dusty, and disappointing. Bad roads and few beaches. So we returned to stay in Los Angeles with friends. Yesterday we drove up the middle of California, very hot and dry, but in the evening we turned east and came up into the mountains of Stanislaus National Forest. Today is sunny and warm and breezy, and we have camped in a beautiful spot along a fork of the Stanislaus River. We are only a few yards from the road, yet the place seems remote. The air is clean; the pine scent, strong; and the stream is cool.

At this moment, we are all taking a therapeutic respite, each in his own way, each in his own direction. The social and physical space of the camper is confining, and while this is beneficial, it becomes cramped and uncomfortable, and we have been on the move for a full week.

The trip has been fatiguing to this point. Travel is trying, especially when it's hot and meals and sleep are irregular. Just the wrong thing for me. This morning I was depressed and felt lonely, so the parting of ways, even momentarily, was painful, but the girls did need a little solitude.

Both Amy and Karen are easy retreaters when stress is present, and they tend to reinforce one another's indulgences that way. I am sure that Karen sometimes feels lost and unable to cope, and fortunately Amy is far enough ahead to see what is taking place but unfortunately not far enough ahead to do much about it. But despite perturbations and various ups and downs, we are doing well after a month.

Last night I was feeling sexually aroused—three nude bodies in a small camper bed will do it every time!—but the girls were tired. They shunned me, perhaps rightly, and suggested

I masturbate. I have no hang-ups about masturbation, and sometimes prefer it when I am tense and uncommunicative, but I did resent it. I resented, not the masturbating (after they were asleep), but the fact that the situation led me to fantasy about another woman.

The girls are still sexually shy with one another. Amy is unsure of Karen's desire for her. Karen said the other day her orgasms were becoming more difficult because she tries to force them and because she is not fantasizing during coitus as she has done with Brian for the last one to two years. Despite their deviance, the girls are still quite inhibited. This is distressing to me. Their bodies should be a great source of joy and delight to themselves, each other, me, and others around us. They cannot yet cope with their freedoms.

Saturday, August 8 The girls returned within fifteen minutes of one another yesterday. Karen arrived first and then bathed nude in the stream in full view, something which considerably aroused me. We had just begun making love when Amy returned, happy and refreshed. We all joined in what was a most satisfying sexual encounter.

Later we had a personal show-and-tell sexual anatomy lesson so that each of us could learn to better please and satisfy the other, appreciating our individual sexual differences. It was very helpful to Amy, who learned most of all that Karen is not so very fragile and sometimes needs even to be roughed a bit and taken, not asked.

Karen has still not written much in her journal. I now feel that rather than procrastinating, she is simply blocked and does not know how to express herself, although she says she is making notes to incorporate later. I wish I could help.

The girls seem happy and relaxed today. They make such pleasant companions for one another, and for me as well, that I should like us to last forever. But even if it should end today, I would judge us each to have grown individually and together in a way that leaves us changed considerably from a mere month ago. We have made our marks on each other.

AMY

Sunday, August 9 I returned Friday to find Rich and Karen making love in the camper. We all felt close again, drawn together rather than straining for a "therapeutic respite," as Rich afterward described our desires for a period of solitude. He had understood, though he had at the time been feeling a conflicting need. I joined them in the camper, and afterward, we had an anatomy lesson, suggested by Karen. A bodily show and tell, pervaded by some modest shyness, of anatomical sensitivity and how we each like to be touched. Karen and I are different. I had found out some time back, with them showing me, and much to my *amazement* and almost disbelief, how hard she liked her breasts caressed; our genital responses differ also. We each showed how we masturbate, techniquewise.

RICH

Sunday, August 9

Walking in the woods.
Picking up favorite things.
Nature feeds the soul.

KAREN

Sunday, August 16 On July 30, we left Palo Alto in a camper packed full of camping gear and headed for Mexico (Baja California) with a brief stop in Los Angeles. We visited Jonathan and Cindy—really beautiful people. I always have a kind of fear grip me just before I meet friends of Rich and Amy, especially people they care about, but my fears were unfounded with Jonathan and Cindy. They were warm and friendly, and I quickly felt at home with them.

Rich had wanted to take LSD while we were in Mexico,

but neither the time nor the place presented itself, so he and Amy took some LSD one afternoon after we had set up camp at Stanislaus. I remember that I heard them discuss it, and then I went down by the brook to get some sun. I felt so alienated and shut out, as though they had gone away, someplace I couldn't go, and that they had left me. Boy! What a scary scene. I thought I had explained to Rich sufficiently my fear of drugs. Oddly enough, *Rich* was the one who warned me about drugs early in our friendship. I had never even smoked marijuana before and at Rich's suggestion read a book which greatly enlightened me. Unfortunately, I had read nothing about psychedelics, nothing except that it changed your chromosomes and caused people to jump out of windows. We had a long discussion which calmed me but left me with many questions and doubts. I consequently have some reading to do on drugs.

RICH

Friday, August 21 The evening was ecstatic and profound, and emotions were running high and flowing freely last night as we three made love in the nicest ways. One must *learn* to make love and enjoy sex with two others, but it comes easily if the mind is open and the heart is full. It was truly group love, with the most rewarding and novel types of combinations imaginable. I've seen many orgies before, a few good ones, and I've even participated from time to time, and I've had sexual experiences with two women several times, but never with such intense feeling, such love.

The girls were beautiful together, too. I enjoy watching them, I must admit, for they can be both delicate and passionate at the same moment, a state of sexual giving and taking which easily eludes the male.

Last night we all went out to dinner and to a San Francisco pornography theater. The films were rather dull. Even in color, they simply lack finesse and good taste. It would be nice to live in a society with really high quality erotic art. Amy and Karen were a combination of bored and amused after half an hour. And the only thing which aroused any of us was a brief scene with two girls, one of them strikingly pretty, in a hayloft. The men were a distinct turnoff. They appeared clumsy. In only one scene was there any indication of a real sexual turn-on, but even that did not lead to an orgasm. And the absence of erotic sounds left things flat and unconvincing. We all agreed that the recorded sound of women making love might well be more stimulating than visual pornography. In any case, we were happy to be able to come home to the real thing.

Wednesday, August 26 We have decided on a course of action that will bring us all closer together. Karen had been offered a job as a secretary in the local branch of the company she used to work for, with an increase in pay. She did not wish to return to the nine-to-five routine and its attendant boredom. I supported this strongly, as it would have meant different schedules and orientations for the coming months, even though she could have saved some money for school in the spring semester. Her registration cannot be officially processed for the fall semester, but she will be able to sit in on the course Amy will be teaching and one other at San Jose State and will get credit during the following semester when she is enrolled. This is a disappointment but hardly a disaster, and I see it as opening other opportunities, especially if she will use her time wisely.

I suggested that she go shopping among the many courses at Stanford a few days a week. She was not too enthusiastic but thought it a good idea. I explained that she could pick and choose among the best lecturers at will, use my faculty library card, etcetera, and generally orient herself to an academic environment and determine her own intellectual interests without pressure. It also means, of course, that she must stimulate and discipline herself in a totally different way, something she has never done before. She will also assume primary responsibility for the household, doing the cleaning, most of the cooking and shopping, and generally managing the house. She will help with typing, filing, some of the finances, and so on and will help me organize the research material for my study of deviance. That way, she will wind up knowing as much as Amy and I about the topic.

So Karen decided not to take the job. This means that we will be supporting Karen, but that is a rather limited way of viewing it, for it will be she who is providing support facilities and services for Amy and me. I am delighted, since it will take some pressure off Amy and still give Karen an opportunity for self-development. In a word, we shall all be living, as Amy and I have, out of a common pot. With respect to our relations, we are becoming, step by step, more integrated and more like a family. We will be more interdependent, with various individual areas of responsibility.

Amy and I will be proud and happy to help pay for Karen's education if we can. I only hope she appreciates and makes the best of it regardless of who pays the bills. Sometimes I wish I were wealthy so that I could buy them whatever their hearts desired, but we are surely fortunate, for we have what we need, plus some things we don't need, in the way of material goods.

After our long discussion over family policy last night, we made love together. Very nice, very satisfying.

Two nights ago, Karen went for dinner and a small party with another student who had been introduced to her by a third party. When she was not home by 12:30–1:00 A.M., I became apprehensive and jealous and could not sleep. I waited up for her, thinking all sorts of thoughts and feeling sorry for myself. When she came in about 3:00 A.M., it was all for nothing. They had sat about drinking and talking, since her date's friends were leaving the country the next day. She had enjoyed herself but had a headache. We talked for a while and then made love. All I needed was reassurance. She has another date tomorrow night, but I don't feel at all jealous about it.

Karen and I go to a Sexual Freedom League marathon encounter all night Friday. It should prove most interesting in a number of ways. I am curious to see how she will react.

We grow closer. I love them both very much.

Monday, August 31 The Sexual Freedom League encounter was rewarding only in that Karen found it mildly interesting and we met a couple who were longtime friends of Jonathan's who were going to look us up soon anyway. The whole thing was run and attended by novices and lacked subtlety. However, those attending made up for it in enthusiasm, and so the evening was passably interesting. We left about 12:30 with Jonathan's friends—they, too, were let down, since they had both been in encounters and sensitivity groups for some time but never sexually oriented ones—and came home to listen to music, talk, and smoke pot. We didn't return for the Saturday session at all.

We were all tired Saturday from lack of sleep (up till 5:00 A.M.), and Amy was cross and bitchy. She experienced for the first time meeting someone whom Karen and I had gotten to know without her. It threw her off a bit, but by evening, we were rested enough to go to a large nude-dancing and -swimming party. The party was relaxed and friendly, and the pool was quite warm and comfortable. We took our acquaintances of the previous evening, and they seemed to fit in well. We all enjoyed the evening.

I found myself stimulated due to a number of attractive women present, and my mood was open, but I made no approaches or advances to any of them. I was more than happy to spend a good part of the time in the pool with Amy and Karen.

A joint and a relaxed conversation in a back bedroom with Amy and Karen and the girl we had invited left me wanting to make love to each of them. I dare say they would have, but Amy especially was still in the process of acquainting herself with Kay. I restrained myself, but it is likely that Kay and I will find ourselves in bed in due course. I certainly hope that won't threaten Amy or Karen. I just feel that she is attractive and interesting and that she might turn out to be a good friend.

Tomorrow is the first day of September. I usually take that date or the Labor Day weekend as signaling the end of vacation and summer and leisure and the start of another academic year, or at least preparations for it. In retrospect, this has indeed been a summer of happiness. Amy and Karen and I have gotten a good start toward a viable three-person marriage. I never really thought we would go so far as to share literally the same bed night after night (a king size in which we sleep sideways, so there is plenty of room), but it is working even at that level of intimacy and cooperation.

A new job for Amy and me, a new graduate program for me, a new undergraduate program for Karen, and a new house and set of friends for us—these things leave us with a lot to explore and experience. But best of all, the search for happiness and fulfillment with each other is proving to be a daily-rewarding task, sometimes trying, sometimes frivolous, but always worth it.

KAREN

Tuesday, September 1 We shared an interesting experience on August 22. We attended a dance in San Francisco sponsored by the Sexual Freedom League and Gay Liberation, among others. What an evening! I had some firsts. I had never seen two men make love; I had never danced with Rich. And we were amused at people's refusal to accept us as a threesome. The three of us would be dancing together, and someone (another guy) would come up and join us, obviously feeling that the threesome needed to be rounded out. Not so; we were having a ball.

Before I came to San Francisco, a friend had written that she wanted me to meet a fellow she respected and admired. She suggested that I contact him when I arrived. When I felt somewhat settled, I did call him. We met once for lunch, and I found him to be a very nice person, enjoyable and interesting to be around, but I foresaw nothing serious between us. Rich was a bit jealous perhaps and maybe anxious, but I convinced him of my intentions, and he seemed agreeable to my seeing George occasionally. George invited me to a potluck dinner with some of his friends, and I had a most enjoyable evening which lasted rather late. When I got home (about 2:30 A.M.), Rich was waiting up for me and was upset and had been worried that I had gone to bed with George. I assured him I hadn't (and in fact didn't have much of an inclination) and tried to calm him down. I think more than being upset that I was out so late, he was more upset over his own reaction. We talked at length and made love. We became closer, more attuned to one another. I must remember to *help* Rich stay tuned in to my feelings, reinforcing my feelings for him to him verbally and discussing my feelings for others. I have seen George four or five times altogether and still have the same feelings now I had to begin with. I want to be his friend and share some pleasant times with him when my schedule and his permit. I think Rich sees the relationship for what it is: platonic friendship.

On August 28, Rich and I attended an encounter group marathon sponsored by the Sexual Freedom League. Amy was busy preparing for her class and elected to stay at home. I had never been in an encounter group, and this sounded like a good initiation. As it turned out, the group was willing and had high expectations, but the planning had been poor and prearrangements almost nil. We did meet one couple, Kay and Randy, who, we found out later, are friends of Jonathan and Cindy. We talked with them awhile and asked them if they'd care to spend the evening at our house, since it appeared the encounter group was a flop. They agreed, and we called Amy to let her know we'd be bringing someone home. Well, as it often happens, two clicked, and everything else was lukewarm. Rich and Kay hit it off fine. I was so-so toward Randy, and Amy felt completely alienated. I felt torn between making Randy feel accepted and further alienating Amy. Rich, Amy, and I ended up making love in the bedroom while Kay and Randy were doing likewise (I think) in the living room. Rich and Kay may get together, but Amy still has some hostile feelings toward Kay, and I feel somewhat shy with Randy. I don't feel sexually inclined, but I would like to be friends. I also feel somewhat of an attraction toward Kay, but I don't know what to do with that.

RICH

Wednesday, September 9 The past weekend was an eventful one, to be sure. We had three couples over on Saturday to take an LSD trip with us. Karen stayed straight but thoroughly enjoyed the evening, and the experience seems to have dispelled many of her fears about the drug. LSD should not be taken lightly or abused, but it can be a powerful therapeutic agent and one means by which to explore inner consciousness as well as interpersonal relations. Everyone, I believe, had a good trip. I felt very close to Amy and Karen, and at one point, we retired to make love. Excruciatingly and indescribably pleasurable!

Later in the evening, I had intercourse with another girl. When I told Karen, she felt hurt and betrayed, but Amy helped there a great deal. By the next day, all seemed to be well.

Karen now sees psychedelic experiences much differently. Before, the only image she had was from those damned sensationalistic news stories and other misleading mass media (not to mention "scientific") input. I am encouraging her to do some reading on the subject, and I think she looks forward to turning on.

Karen's former boss and lover is in town and visited this morning. I didn't talk to him, but I don't feel jealous of him at all at this point. She has a date with another man, but I feel no jealousy there either. I am growing more secure with her and hope to be able to share her as I do Amy.

Amy is busy preparing her course for the fall. It looks like it will be a good one, with some interesting twists for the students. She is feeling more confidence as she structures and organizes the material. I am proud of the way she is handling it.

Thursday, September 10 Another stroke of good fortune: One of Amy's professors called today to tell her that she has been hired as a teaching assistant. This for all intents and purposes solves the immediate financial uncertainties and means we can cover all expenses though next June or so without the necessity of Karen taking a nonacademic job.

I am really proud of Amy. I don't think she would have gone knocking on the doors if I had not pushed her to do so, even though she is obviously qualified. Perhaps she may be a teacher yet.

KAREN

Sunday, September 13 On September 5, we invited over what was to be a few couples, but grew into more than a few, so one couple could teach us some massage techniques. Rich also wanted to take a trip, and the party was intended to give me a chance to be around people who were taking LSD to see how they act, etcetera. Everything went great until Rich and I went downstairs and made love. Amy joined us, and Rich went back upstairs. Amy and I had a nice talk, and I got a beautiful breast massage. Wow! Anyway, when we went upstairs, Rich was making love (or had just finished) to Kay. Jeez! The old fears came out again in full force. Not that he was making love to Kay. I had expressed my liking for her and my unthreatened feelings, but it was sort of like Rich wasn't satisfied with me and as soon as Amy came down to take over and keep me occupied then he went after what he really wanted in the first place. Chalk that up to my insecurities, I suppose. But I do like Kay and don't mind Rich seeing and making love to her.

I've had a few outings with old friends. I've told none of them of my group marriage and don't know how I'll go about it when I do. Rich questions me about my "social stability"; I'm not sure I have any of that, whatever it is. I resent sometimes his requiring me to classify my relationships with others. I don't mind exploring them with him; I enjoy discussing various reactions and feelings I have. I know I have a tendency to withdraw, particularly when I'm caught up in my own schedule, and I appreciate the way Rich tries to pull me out, so to speak. But I resent him trying to fit me and my needs into a mold. This is something we must work on together so that we feel comfortable when for one reason or another we aren't able to satisfy a certain need in the other (for example, my need for aloneness).

AMY

Sunday, September 13 I teach my first class Thursday, and that is foremost in my thoughts. I'm scared but excited about it. It is a challenge and a chance to grow, personally and professionally, but it is the risk-taking that always scares me. I am self-conscious in front of people and have nothing in my past experience to reassure me that I am capable of talking for the length of a class period, in this case a two-and-a-half-hour class! I don't think I have ever in my entire life spoken continuously for fifteen minutes straight without silences or interjections. The problem I had in the beginning with taped letters was the sheer novelty (difficulty) of piling so many sentences one after another without someone else saying something for a break. I have a small feeling deep down inside that I will do all right and probably even enjoy myself, but in the forefront of my mind is the nagging fear, "But what if I don't—?"

Karen will be one of my students. I feel good about that. If Rich were there, I would feel too self-conscious and embarrassed. I don't know quite why, perhaps my inferiority feelings. But Karen seems to understand my fears, perhaps because we are so much alike. She will empathize if I make a fool of myself and console and comfort me. Rich would comfort and support me, but he could not as fully empathize because of our personality differences. Rich is like another half to me in a complementary way, while Karen is like another internal half. A true sister, perhaps, in the sense of two of a kind. If we seem to overstate our similarities sometimes, it is only because there seems such an amazing number of them and they just overshadow the differences. Probably just because we naturally expected a lot more differences than there have turned out to be.

We are all at home with each other more, comfortable and familiar with day-to-day living together and being each other's home. Home to me has always been wherever Rich is, rather than a place or house; and now Karen is becoming a part of that, too. We all feel it when we are together in a larger social group, like at a party. There's a special comfortableness and identification when the three of us come back together in the midst of social mingling; somehow we keep ending up seeking each other out to relax with. We're really a lot like newlyweds socially. I'm afraid our closeness sometimes makes others feel excluded.

Karen has learned what it means to see people as straight, at the same time realizing that she is becoming less so herself and feeling glad about that. She's seeing this after getting together with previously close friends; she's finding them nowhere near so relaxed, happy, growing, etcetera, as we are. She's beginning to see the conventional world from the standpoint of being a little outside of it. She has become aware of how abrasive the world outside our door is in comparison with our private world. To go out and try to run errands is to come home bruised and battered—by the traffic, smells, dirt in the air, incompetence, insensitivity, disregard, etcetera, that are so pervasive. Seeing these things for herself, Karen can now understand Rich and me better.

RICH

Monday, September 21 Two days ago, we had our first group psychedelic experience, and it was a very strange and wonderful experience to be sure. It was painful, rewarding, expanding, confusing, enlightening, and valuable. The only mistake we made was that we did not all take the same substance. I took mescaline and thus had a slower, longer, deeper trip; Karen and Amy took small amounts of LSD and went up quickly, but not so far.

The primary effect, other than some rather pleasant visual and bodily reactions, was a blurring and softening of social and sexual roles. An important effect on Karen was that it released a combination, often in rapid succession, of joy and fear along with some hostility and vindictiveness. None of us expected it and, thus, were all surprised by it. It did blow her mind somewhat. Word meanings were unclear, even to the speakers. Emotions seemed to hang and float in the air, and Karen could see the misunderstanding and panic on my face when she attacked me. This hostility toward me also alienated Amy. But it was not intentional; it simply was there as a kind of interpersonal energy which the drug released, exactly as it is supposed to do.

Karen did open up a great deal, perhaps more than ever before. This too may have threatened Amy because Karen let go in an hour or two what Amy has taken months and many trips to do. Karen said she now knows what hiding (evading, deflecting, avoiding) means and what it means to come out and play (interact with fidelity to self and sensitivity to others) even if it leads to some conflict.

We all agreed that the masculine sides or aspects of Karen and Amy were displayed. My own feminine characteristics may have been there also. I suggested that for all intents and purposes other than reproduction, biology may be an accident to the soul or self and that sex is a concept properly applied to personal development and social interaction and cultural participation. We may have briefly traded roles. In any case, we *all* know now from experience that we are larger and more complex than our conscious and rational actions alone would indicate. Amy and I knew it from previous trips, but now we have shared it. We *know* that there is more to the Rich-Amy-Karen game than meets the merely rational part of the mind's eye.

We agreed that future psychedelic excursions are in order in due time, when we have digested this one and are ready to explore further. Karen was fascinated as well as confused by the experience. She had been listening to Amy and me carefully all along and was prepared to come out and wanted to do so. Amy and I both were caught a little flat-footed, and I kept going up, up, up, slowly but surely, for four to six hours. Amy had to slow me down with tranquilizers about six hours into the trip so that I could cope with Karen. And Amy was alienated when Karen and I stayed up until 4:30 A.M. to talk. She felt as though she were left out. She was not.

The relationship between Amy and Karen also became a matter for discussion. They admitted they were clearly sexually attracted to one another but that they do not know how to make advances toward one another; that is, they do not know what role to play or what is appropriate for each of them. It was a good trip in the sense that we really did expand our awareness of one another. I am left with a new kind of respect and appreciation for Karen. Not only did she participate; she, to some extent unwittingly, became the center of attraction. She discovered new types of experience, new levels of awareness, new dimensions of meaning. She grew. We all grew, with our own selves, with one another. Despite confusion, the bonds were cemented a little more securely.

On Sunday, we were all tired, and Amy was still feeling a little alienated. I worried and wondered how to get the two of them back together. I became frustrated and took a walk, which was both a physical and emotional release. Karen felt pressured because her mother and another man had called saying how lonely they felt and placing heavy emotional loads on her. She was depressed in the evening. However, a night's sleep and a beautiful morning have restored each of us. But we each know that we have only tapped the surface of our collective self.

Amy gave her first lecture last Thursday. I was very proud of her. Karen said she did quite well. She has a class of twelve, which is good because she feels she can manage a small class on her first foray as a teacher. Karen taped it and presented it to me as a present from Amy.

I love them.

RICH

Wednesday, September 23 I don't always know what to make of Karen's actions. Sometimes they confuse and upset me; sometimes I don't think she knows what and why and fails to see the effects of her actions on others.

Tuesday she went to visit a man she had met about a week ago. She had visited his apartment once before, only to get mauled by his advances, which, at that point, she refused. She found him sexually attractive and intellectually stimulating. He is fairly new to the area, hence lonely and horny, and I suppose he saw Karen as an opportunity to satisfy those needs. Day before yesterday, they made love. She says that the sexual experience was quite good but that there was not much emotional rapport or communication between them.

I wonder, of course, what she wants from him and fear what and how much he will demand from her. And I am uncertain what his effect might be on the three of us. Both Amy and Karen assure me that the whole thing is consistent with our open marriage ethic. However, there is the possibility that he and Karen are merely exploiting one another, and there was a certain impulsiveness about her actions. Also, it is possible that she is simply testing her various limits with me, to find out where and how I will stop her, and/or that she is getting a certain kind of emotional vengeance for the fact that a week and a half ago I went to a party with another female friend and had intercourse with two girls during the evening.

I do not regard her actions as a threat to the existence or even general stability of the marriage, but it is producing some anxiety for me and has an effect on group composure. I simply think the man will make too many demands, some of which may conflict with our group efforts. He knows of her involvement and apparently winced a little at it but is satisfied with the situation. I don't necessarily want her to stop seeing him, but I do wish she would be a little more considerate of my feelings in the matter.

Her interest may be partly due to the fact that he is black, and although she has admitted a curiosity about sex with Negroes which dates back to high school, this was her first sexual encounter with a black man. That fact doesn't upset me particularly, though it requires some acclimation. Karen says she wants him to meet us and wants us all to be friends. I am for it but fear that he will be both cocky and tense.

The whole thing led to considerable discussion yesterday and left us all feeling worn and tired. I'm not sure what will happen next. Karen is planning to audit a course he is teaching once a week, but I am not sure whether that is to guarantee a meeting or to sustain and develop an intellectual interest.

Karen says I still control the relationship in that if I asked her not to see him again, she would comply. But I don't want her compliance; I want voluntary moves on her part because she reads my personality, if anything at all. I am *not* sorry or angry; indeed, it may be that by learning to share her this way, we will all grow, and I will be able to eliminate my jealousy feelings and build up my trust. For, after all, Karen has learned honesty. She conferred with Amy beforehand, told me about meeting him and everything subsequent to that. When she confided her sexual encounter to me Tuesday afternoon, I became very aroused, and we had some very nice lovemaking ourselves.

I still do not want to curtail her freedom. It is wrong to do so and unnecessary in a marriage, provided that there is another, deeper level of fidelity and trust, provided the outside party's expectations and demands are not damaging or do not cause conflict within. Amy and I call this *primary allegiance.* I am uncertain about it with Karen, although I have forgone several episodes and opportunities with current friends and lovers just so she would not feel threatened or jealous.

I would much prefer to weather these little emotional storms easily and quickly, though I refuse to deny my negative emotions some appropriate means of expression. And I am convinced from my experiences with Amy that even if I fail to do so, to make the attempt is quite worth the effort. Jealousy is destructive. I sometimes feel it is healthy in a symptomatic way, since it affords a mediocre and unclear guarantee of interest, but the emotion itself is fruitless and aggravating.

Karen says she would enjoy going to bed with this man and me together. She contends that part of her motive is to find a male playmate for me for sexual and intellectual purposes. If so, that is more than gracious and understanding of her, but that could be a rationalization of her own behavior, which I sometimes see as threatening to me.

Amy is pained by my upset. She says I have nothing to fear but my own worries. She is credible and trustworthy on the point, so I want to believe her but am confused and ambivalent. Karen says the relationship is not crucial and that her motivation is to make a new friend and share him with us without altering the emotional life of the group. I hope she knows herself well enough to ascertain that, and I hope she is telling the truth. A lie or even a distortion at this point on this delicate and touchy subject could have many undesirable consequences.

KAREN

Sunday, September 27 September 15, school began! Whew! Amy and I drove to San Jose for various meetings for her and so I could get a look at the campus. Among other things, I met a fellow, Andy, who interested me for various reasons (his mannerism, his self-confidence, etcetera), among them that he was black. He asked if he could call me, and I said yes. He did call, and it turns out he is from Puerto Rico and had just come here from Atlanta, where he taught for two years. I discussed my interests in Andy with Rich. We sort of explored them together. I admitted I wasn't sure what my feelings were; perhaps I was just curious because he's black. Anyway, Rich was open and responsive to me; one concern was what effect, if any, there would be if I should become involved with Andy, since he is teaching at San Jose State. Also, would there be any ripples if he should reveal our group marriage to anyone?

So after several long phone conversations, I stopped by Andy's one day to visit on my way to do some errands. Well, boy, was he different! He completely threw me, and it scared me away. He called and apologized several times, so I agreed to meet him and chat. We had a nice long talk and agreed to "start over again." Rich was apprehensive because I had told him what happened at Andy's the first time, but I again discussed my feelings and curiosities, and Rich and I both ended up feeling better.

Apart from this, we all seemed to be in an especially good mood, and Rich said he wanted to take another trip with the little bit of acid we had left from the party. I happened to be in the right mood; I had been reading Leary's *Politics of Ecstacy* and was feeling pretty daring, I suppose, and agreed to take my first trip. Rich took a capsule of mescaline, and Amy and I took what was left of the LSD, which amounted to really very small doses.

My trip was what could be described as a heavy trip. It wasn't colors and lights and geometric designs but was centered on my relationship with Rich and Amy. All things considered, it was a good trip. I've never before had the experience of really being inside my mind! Rich took a different drug and so had some trouble tuning in to where I was, but anyway, the most important outcome, aside from the intense interpersonal closeness I felt among the three of us, was that Rich and I had our first confrontation. We locked horns; it was a contest, a display of wills, and we realized our deep commitment to each other and perhaps (as we later interpreted it) a bit of competitiveness over Amy. The second important outcome was that I told Rich that one of the reasons I had become interested in Andy was that I was looking for a playmate for him, intellectually first and sexually if possible. I saw in Andy some of the mental sharpness I had seen so often in Rich. And I had heard Rich say, "It gets pretty lonely up here sometimes," meaning that it's hard to find male friends who are able to stimulate him intellectually and with whom he can communicate at a deep level. I don't pretend even to be at his level, and in all probability, I never will. But I do recognize his need, and I would delight in being able to present to him another mind of his caliber.

We spent all evening and into the morning coming down —and whew! What total exhaustion one feels. Sunday was spent recuperating; Rich and I napped, and then we had a party. It was just the three of us, and we tried hard to be gay, but Amy and I were feeling some hostilities as a result of the trip. Amy resented me hurting Rich, and then I felt betrayed that I had been completely open and defenseless and now, the next day, what I had revealed was being thrown in my face.

We all talked and tried to examine each other's feelings. Amy and I discussed our feelings, and our ultimate conclusion was that we are truly committed to each other and the group because none of us can stand the other being hurt. We are so intertwined and deeply involved that it is no longer an experiment or a trial marriage. It's the real thing, baby!

School became a reality, and Amy needed all the support and reinforcement Rich and I could muster. She's the sexiest teacher *I've* ever had!

After discussing my feelings inside and out, I decided to go see Andy. I discussed the matter with Amy before I left the house. I wanted not to hurt or slight Rich in any way; I wanted to be as considerate of him as I possibly could. Amy said she thought I couldn't be any more considerate than I had been and that I should feel free to do whatever I felt like and that I shouldn't be so overly concerned that I become entangled in my concerns. Well, I *did* go see Andy, and we did make love. I enjoyed our lovemaking, and my curiosities were satisfied.

Rich at this time was having difficulty of sorts and viewed Andy as a threat, especially after I told him I had made love with Andy. We had many talks, and just when I thought Rich had worked out his feelings, he'd get to feeling depressed and threatened again. We later learned it could be attributed to a great extent to some new prescribed pills Rich had begun taking. They relaxed him, but at the same time slightly depressed him to the point where he couldn't handle social situations well, especially ones potentially threatening to him.

Finally, Rich took off one afternoon to do some errands. When he returned, he said he had stopped to see Andy to explain he *wanted* to be able to share me, that he didn't want to compete, and to tell Andy he wants to get to know him. Fortunately or unfortunately, Andy wasn't home. The fact that he wasn't there and Rich didn't actually get to talk to him is beside the point. The most important thing to me is that Rich made the effort to get things off on the right foot with Andy. As it turned out, I invited Andy over for a quiet evening which was very enjoyable. Rich liked him; Amy did, too. He came over a few days later for a TV special, and again, we had a nice day. Rich still feels a bit tender about Andy. I suppose with time he'll see my loyalties and my commitment are to him and to Amy and to the three of us. Sometimes I feel deceived to a degree. Rich keeps asking if I'd be doing such and such if we were married. Well, we *are* married, only not in the conventional way. I always admired the freedom of Rich and Amy's marriage. I began to feel as though I had been invited to partake of something but not been told the rules until after I had done what I thought was acceptable.

I realize now that Rich and I need to work out our feelings over these new relationships just as he and Amy had to. I also know that Rich feels very secure in his relationship with Amy. Not because they're legally married, but because he knows how deeply committed she is to him (and he to her). Rich and I haven't had the time to build up the secure feelings, but we will because the basis of our feelings is strong and enduring.

This cold I have is really getting to me. Gad! I had planned to go to class with Andy Wednesday. My cold was in full swing then, so I had to cancel attending his class so I'd be able to attend my regular class the following day. While we had discovered the reasons for Rich's reactions, he still was feeling unsure of my relationship with Andy. I was beginning to wonder about everything. I couldn't understand Rich's pressures for me to define my relationship with Andy. I view it as intellectually stimulating, culturally interesting, and sexually enjoyable. I also want Rich and Andy to become friends, but I have no long-term arrangement with or commitment to Andy. I get frustrated when Rich pushes me beyond what I consider reasonable limits in trying to explain my interest in Andy. I know that a great deal of Rich's reaction stems from his sexual feelings for me and from his unresolved homosexual curiosities. I'm trying to cope with him on those levels without alienating Andy. Whew!

While I am deeply committed to Rich and Amy and us, I still have feelings for others. I want to see my old friends occasionally, and I want to be friends with Andy. I also know he is lonely. He is new here and hasn't met many people. Having experienced a great deal of loneliness in Dallas, I'm especially empathetic to this.

RICH

Friday, October 2 Things have not gone so well with Karen. My jealousies keep cropping up in the face of what I see as a chronic tendency to explore outside our family. This may or may not be destructive to us, but she doesn't seem to me to be giving me time to digest these explorations of hers. Hence, I question her motives and her priorities. I always fear that she may be seeking her own man, but she denies this, saying she already has one in me. I feel she is not doing anything wrong but just being insensitive to my reactions. Yesterday, the phone rang at least six or eight times for her with calls from three men making demands of various kinds on her. I want her to be free and happy and fulfilled, but right now I RESENT IT, and her involvements indicate to me that she does not really feel married to me and to Amy. For example, one fellow called to ask her to a dinner a week and a half from now. She accepted without asking at all if we, as a family, might have other plans. Amy would never do this without at least a brief consultation.

I don't object to *what* Karen is doing, but rather *how* she is going about it. Perhaps she does not wish to be as close, as integrated, as involved with me as Amy has been and is. I should take that into account if it is true. But she has said repeatedly that she has never loved anyone so much, shared so much, or spent so much time with anyone as she has with me. Perhaps I should be satisfied with what I have and not complain about her outside relationships. This, however, will force me to pull back a little emotionally in order to defend myself, for I have indeed left myself very much exposed to her. That's why it hurts.

Karen, ill with a head cold, has been weak and low. What bothers me is that instead of letting Amy and me care for and pamper her a little, she withdrew physically and emotionally. This hurt, too. It makes me see that sometimes she doesn't know how to let someone love her.

Next week, I begin classes and teaching. We shall have less playtime together but must cooperate more than ever in order to function individually and as a group. I hope the summer honeymoon has helped prepare us. I feel as though whatever the problems, the initial phases of our marriage are a success.

Monday, October 5 After a hectic and traumatic weekend, involving a serious misunderstanding and dispute between Karen and me, classes began for me today. I feel good about them, look forward to putting my mind in gear again.

But I am presently occupied by the events of the weekend. I often feel that my comments in this journal fail to do justice to the complexities, the subtleties, the dynamics and the total motivation and so on of our interaction. This is such a case. So many things were going on. Some small details proved of critical importance. The most important thing about it is that while it was a blowup and could have led to far worse than it did, it has been handled well, and we are now much more in control. Harmony has returned. We've done a lot of forgiving. And the fact that we are *three* in number was also critical at several points. It definitely was a help to have Amy serving as a mediator, an umpire, an emotional go-between for Karen and me.

Jason, Karen's old boss and lover, was in town for the

weekend and wanted Karen to stay with him. Karen didn't have deep feelings for him anymore, and besides, she was sick from a cold, cramps from her period were coming on, and she was tired. Also, I was less than enthusiastic about the idea, although I had no objection to her seeing him or even making love with him inasmuch as I do not see him as a threat. They met Friday for an early dinner but did not, for several reasons, hit it off well. Thus, as Karen explained it, they terminated the relationship because they had alienated one another.

On the same evening, we had been invited to a party at the home of a couple who have a heated swimming pool. Amy was tired, but a swim sounded relaxing, so I went, leaving approximately thirty minutes before Karen came home, thirty minutes which would have substantially altered subsequent events. At the party, I had intercourse with a girl who makes Karen feel particularly jealous. I had abstained with this girl for some time for just that reason, though I could internally guarantee that she was no threat to my emotional relationship with Karen. She was, however, a close friend of long standing. Perhaps Karen was testing my responsiveness to her feelings through this woman, for even Karen could give no specific reason as to why she felt jealous. At this party, I went to bed with Maggie, which proved a pleasant sexual reunion but hardly one that would keep me from returning home or one that would draw me away from Karen. The fact that Karen was out with Jason may have entered my mind, but it was not a crucial factor. The fact that Karen had been seeing three different men off and on, having sex with two of them, and seemingly not responding to or being sensitive to my jealous feeling, may have been subconsciously crucial. For the most part, I simply felt like relaxing at the party and with Maggie, and I did.

As it turned out, of course, Karen had come home rather early, had not had a good time, and was feeling rather badly. She and Amy—and two other girls who were in town visiting

us, one a long-term friend and lover of mine whom Karen
likes and enjoys—had a long and enjoyable talk. Everybody
was in bed asleep when I came home, so I knew nothing of
Karen's evening.

The next evening I had planned to have a few couples over
to listen to a special quadraphonic broadcast. The few couples swelled into a very mixed group of about twenty, and so
became a party, and so also spoiled listening to the broadcast
despite the presence of much audio equipment. Earlier in the
day, Karen said she was afraid it would turn into a big
"screwing party"; but this was a projection of her fears,
partly inspired by the fact that Maggie and another girl
Karen doesn't care for were coming.

I told Karen about the previous night with Maggie. She
related rather sadly the events with Jason. She did not react
when I said I had gone to bed with Maggie, but it got under
her skin and stayed there, the jealousy apparently eating
away at her. She mentioned this twice later in the afternoon
and asked if she was expected to play hostess that evening.
I said no, but to do what she felt like doing. She was getting
more uptight all the time.

The party was friendly and relaxed, and while the concert
was somewhat spoiled, I enjoyed seeing everyone. It did
become something of a sex party, although not by design.
Maggie and another fellow came and took an LSD trip and
retired to our bedroom shortly thereafter. Karen stayed in
her room, coming out only briefly, with a fake smile plastered
on her face. Two or three persons asked me what was bothering her. I struggled to listen to the concert over the chatter
and after a while took two girls (both of whom are exploring
bisexuality) upstairs.

Karen had said she didn't think she belonged this evening.
And at one point, she thought she saw me in the bedroom
with Maggie sprawled nude on the bed. She was mistaken,
but that error in perception caused her to leave without
telling anyone. I didn't know she had left until I saw her car

was gone. But I knew where she had gone: to Andy's, her new black lover. I had never had anyone pull such a stunt on me, especially not a wife, and so I was hurt. Of course, I did not know how jealous she felt of Maggie nor that she had made a case of mistaken identity at a particularly bad moment. Perhaps she *wanted* to see me with Maggie to justify her anger and her desire to leave.

I was feeling very jealous of Andy late in the evening. The party had spoiled my concert, and Karen had spoiled my evening. I was tempted to go get her but restrained myself and went to bed with Amy. I felt that she had gone to Andy either in desperation and anger or to hurt me. In the latter, she succeeded temporarily; but the next day, she denied that this was her intention. Andy was aware that she had come to him because of her own insecurities and told her so. Karen came home late and slept by herself.

The next day was icy. No communication at all. Amy counseled me to wait until Karen got sufficiently in command to bring the matter up. In the afternoon, she did. We talked, sometimes angrily and heatedly, for about an hour. Amy felt somewhat alienated herself but tried to mediate the discussion. The thing I was most hurt by was, not the fact that Karen had left us or that she had fucked with Andy, but rather her cynicism when we talked. It was her way of covering her own hurt, a way to hold back tears.

But, fortunately, we did talk, and we did smooth things out. We resolved the conflict, rather quickly and efficiently under the circumstances. Most married couples would let something like this drag on for a week or more of backbiting, snide remarks, and so on. Sunday night we were tired, and classes began the next day (today), so we went to sleep rather early.

Today Karen and I embraced several times, apologized to one another (she admitted that she was not a very good fighter), and we came to good terms. We did not sweep the issue under the rug, but neither did it become acute. The whole business was the result of bad timing and several errors in judgment. At the same time that Karen was withdrawing from both Jason *and* Andy (for she said she had decided to suspend things with Andy until I worked out my feelings and until she and I had built a more solid foundation of trust and communication which would allow more freedom), I made the mistake (in context) of having sex with Maggie. Just when Karen was going to abstain from activities which were threatening to *me,* I indulged in activities which were threatening to her. Bad timing.

One result of all of this—a strange one—is that I see Andy as less of a threat and more of a friend because even though he had Karen sexually, he realized and explored her motives with her. He was a friend to her when she needed someone to talk with and someone to reassure and embrace her. That is, I do not see him exploiting her. He is lonely, too—new in Palo Alto, new job, many pressures, far from home. I was sympathetic, but I feared he would want too much from Karen. Now I think perhaps not. I want to be able to share her according to her wishes, her standards, and her values, which must of course to some extent be compatible with mine. Somehow, in this case, Andy's sympathetic and yet critical response leaves me with more respect for him. Karen said he is a good lover. I had analyzed my fearfulness with regard to this as being partly due to the lack of a firm emotional base with Karen and partly due to my battered physical self-image as a result of the skiing accident and the ensuing multiple illnesses. That is, I have not *felt* so terribly virile, although it seems in fact I'm doing quite well. Oddly, again, it was primarily through conversations with Maggie that I discovered this self-image problem as the basis of my feelings about Andy. Actually, I should be and often am pleased when Amy and Karen have pleasant, fulfilling experiences, even, perhaps especially, sexual ones. I hardly feel inadequate when I am feeling up to par. After discussing it with

Maggie, I communicated this to Amy and Karen. It turns out this was much of the reason Karen was going to cool things off—for me, until I felt better, believing that the jealous feelings would subside as I felt stronger.

The most remarkable thing is that while it is not over in any definitive sense, we were able to manage it, the three of us, working together, helping one another to understand, to communicate, to express, to feel.

I have learned some things about Karen's tolerance limits, and she has learned that she does not express negative feelings very well. *That*—and not whether A fucked B, or C saw a threat to B while doing X with A, or anything of that sort —is what is important. There will be more conflict; there will be distorted perceptions in the future; there will be difficult situations, and so on; but the key issue will be whether we can manage, negotiate, and resolve each difficulty as it arises, learning what we can about each other in the process and learning about the process itself. That requires maturity, good will, and love.

Saturday, October 10 Three months of this deviant style of life has caused us to leave our marks on one another, probably for life, regardless of our eventual outcome. We are, I believe, *transforming* one another to some extent. Partly it is a result of the necessary give-and-take of daily living. Partly it is new discoveries we make in one another. Partly it is the hurts and disappointment, the pain as well as the pleasure we bear and give to one another. And partly it is each one's simple acceptance and appreciation of the talents, limits, and traits of the others. We have not lived up to all the expectations we had of one another, but then it is characteristic of those who explore and experiment not to find everything they seek. Still, it is folly to expect less rather than more of one's lovers and companions. To expect less than they are capable of is to insult them. And the person who sets his own goals too low has as his only satisfaction easy success.

This is not at all to say that we three are failing, only that we are coming more and more- -or so I feel—to accept one another as we are; this makes it easier to be *what* or *who* you are, even if one is idealistic, as I am, about one's own self. Another way of saying it might be to say simply that I am more and more comfortable with Amy and Karen.

Classes at Stanford began this week for Amy and me. And Karen is finding a greater need for reading time and study. She has enrolled in a weekly encounter group, which should make for interesting results. My teaching assistantship is ideal for my current status and interests. I am interested in the material, and I only hope I communicate my enthusiasm to the students.

The result of these recent schedules means more structure, more routine, and less time, particularly less spontaneous action, together. It has its good points, of course, but I do enjoy playing, talking, walking, or making love with Amy and Karen. They both feel stiff challenges with school. And they both tire easily, as I expect of women. No, they are not weaker, but they do have more little tasks, expend more energy, and thus need more rest and sleep. Under those circumstances, having two wives makes excellent sense. I sometimes wear them out with what can only be called too much life. But, to be honest, I must say they each are quite spunky and independent.

Life without either of them would be quite different, not impossible, not necessarily unhappy, but definitely quite different.

Sunday, October 11 Amy came downstairs to watch a movie on TV with me, but somehow we felt out of touch with one another. She felt I was bottling her up. This struck me as odd and sad because I have been feeling that I was appreciating her more and paying more attention to the things she tells me.

Karen is tired and busy this evening and is upstairs reading.

I feel very lonely and depressed. And I am sure there are

a number of things bothering each of them that I cannot get at. Perhaps it is only the result of the added pressures of school. Amy has mentioned several times how she is unsure of herself regarding the assumption of further classes next week. Maybe we needed a longer honeymoon. Whatever it is, I feel lonely and alienated.

KAREN

Sunday, October 11 One big hang-up for me, and one I need and want to overcome but which I seem to keep fighting, is this pressure to grow. I want to know myself and genuinely like myself, but I keep hitting snags, keep falling behind. I feel as though I'm causing Rich and Amy to slow down, to backtrack, on *my* account. I keep reminding myself they have been together eight years and have been through some rough times working their feelings out. They, naturally, know each other better, their moods and tolerance levels, too. We spend virtually all our time together, and especially now with the pressures of school, I feel the need to take a breather occasionally. I seem to need time to sort out my feelings and reasonings and reactions. I need time alone, to think or write or read, but *alone.* Rich seems to gain strength from people; I seem to need my solitude.

Rich has such a strong personality and has a tendency to push on Amy and me. Amy resists better than I do. I seem to let myself get pushed in a corner before I react. I need to develop my own rate of growth, my own pace, and ask Rich to help keep me going instead of him forcing his pace on me. I simply can't keep up, and as I see myself falling further and further behind, I panic.

I have been asked my motivations for entering into my relationship with Rich and Amy. I must admit, the first time it was asked, I was at a loss for words. It seems so simple and so clear to me. Why does anyone get married? I love them; their happiness is important to me. I want to share my life and love with them. I'm so fortunate to be loved by two people. I'm so lucky to have a companion, friend, and lover such as Amy, especially since I've never been really close to another girl. And Rich—he's more than any woman could ask for. I feel so inadequate at times, and the frustration comes because I restrain myself from showing my feelings. I'm still a bit shy about approaching Amy sexually—and Rich sometimes, too.

Back in September, Jason and his wife had come here for a vacation of sorts, and Jason had called me and stopped by very briefly to say hello. He told me he'd be coming back to Palo Alto the first of October and would I be able to see him. I said yes and left it at that.

When Jason called last week, we agreed to meet for an early dinner. The evening started out pleasant enough, but as it progressed, it got progressively worse. Jason and I didn't hit it off. We ended our relationship, though Jason said he still loves me and feels committed to me and would be there to help should I ever need him. I was feeling pretty crummy and decided while I was out, I might as well go clarify some things with Andy. While driving down El Camino Real, I glanced at the car next to me at a stoplight, and there was Andy. We sat in the car, and I tried to explain that I was interested in him and in pursuing our relationship but that my first concern was Rich and he needed my help in working out some feelings right now. I didn't want to stop seeing him

(Andy), but neither could I expect him to wait for me; so I'd understand if he would simply cut things off now. We decided to just wait and see. I went on home and related the whole sequence of events to Amy. I had just missed Rich. He had decided to go to a party with Abe and Maggie and had left only minutes before I arrived home.

I was feeling let down because of what had transpired between Jason and me but relieved that I had squared things away with Andy. Our weekend guests came in, and we all sat around the table and had a nice long girl-talk chat, then went to bed. Rich came home about 3:00 A.M. The following day, I related what had happened to him, and he was sad about Jason, about the way it happened. While we sat there talking, he began telling me about the party and said he had made love to Maggie, that she "seduced" him. My first reaction was just hurt. The one person by whom (for some stupid reason) I feel threatened, the one person I had asked him *not* to take to bed—*that's* the person he does make love to!

This was Saturday morning, and that evening we had planned to listen to a special broadcast with two or three couples. Well, that somehow grew all out of proportion, and we ended up with a real party on our hands.

By the time guests began arriving, I felt totally alienated from Rich. I sat in my room reading, and when I finally went out, the living room was wall-to-wall people. Amy said later I looked like a frightened animal when I sat down. That's the way I felt, too, like a stranger, though I knew almost everyone there. I wandered around trying to look as though I belonged, but I didn't pull it off too well. As the evening went on, I felt worse; Rich and I had words, and I definitely wasn't in the mood for a party. I went to his study and had just fallen asleep when our guests came into change for the party. Amy came in shortly thereafter, and the four of us sat talking for over an hour. That perked up my spirits, and we all trekked into the kitchen for food. My high spirits didn't last long; again the party scene made me feel like an outsider.

Several of those present were nude by this time, and for some reason that threatened me, too. I was really in bad shape mentally and emotionally. The one person I should have been able to turn to—Amy (who I knew wasn't having a great time either)—I couldn't. I don't know why, and I've since given it a lot of thought.

I walked toward my room, which was occupied, and detoured to the bathroom. As I walked by, I glanced into the bedroom (the door was slightly ajar) and saw a man, who I thought was Rich, and Maggie. I went on into the bathroom and composed myself, then went to the guest room. The door was locked, and there were voices inside. (I later learned it was Rich *there.*) Disgusted, frustrated, and hurt, I went back to my room, found it empty, sat down, and tried to think. Whatever reasoning I tried to use, one thing was obvious: I was uncomfortable and out of place, so I decided to go out. I slipped past the "partiers", got in my car, and started to drive to nowhere in particular. I ended up at an all-night restaurant having hot chocolate and reading for an hour or so. I decided to take a drive to the city to just drive out my tension, but halfway there I turned around and came back, having decided that Rich certainly wasn't denying himself any physical pleasures, so why the hell should I! I drove over to Andy's apartment talking to myself, reasoning, examining, questioning.

I spent two or three hours with Andy. He was understanding and helpful. We made love several times, and I left in the wee hours. There were still some people from the party camped on the living room floor when I got home. I tiptoed through and quietly slipped into bed in my room. Whew! What a nightmare of a weekend.

Sunday I slept quite late; our house guests had gone by the time I emerged from my room. I fixed myself toast and coffee and tried to concentrate on studying, but no chance. I was so upset, I decided to get the confrontation over with; so I picked Amy up on the way, and we joined Rich, who was watching a ball game on TV.

We had a jim-dandy argument. Rich felt sorry about the party but could not see any justification for my actions. I couldn't stand the conflicting feelings inside. On top of the issue at hand, I don't fight well; so I resort to being cynical, which throws Rich into a fit of rage. Amy tried to be the buffer, but her patience is not limitless either. We ended up with nothing resolved, lots of hurt feelings, and everyone alienated. I began to doubt whether or not I belonged, whether or not I really fit in. So many things seemed paradoxical to me, and my head was ready to burst with so many things I couldn't seem to reconcile. We ended up just backing off.

I tried to study but couldn't concentrate. Amy came up a short time later and asked me to trust her, to come to her, to let her help. We both ended up crying and, ultimately, feeling better. As though enough hadn't happened, my period started; I had cramps from late afternoon on. I fell asleep with the heating pad and was wakened by Amy about 11:00 P.M.

I undressed and went straight to bed.

School started for Rich on Monday (October 5), so we never fully discussed the happening of the weekend. Feelings between Rich and I improved and grew warmer. It's impossible to keep your distance with someone you love. We came to a unanimous conclusion: The weekend had been a comedy of bad timing.

The one recurrent theme, the resounding truth that keeps cropping up, is us, the importance of the three of us, our love for each other, and the fact that we are unable, as a unit or as individuals, to function when there is friction or hurt. Our emotions are so interlocked.

For Rich, getting back into school is like a good swim after working in the hot sun all day. That isn't to say he didn't enjoy his summer, but he had been concerned as to whether he could handle school and all its pressures. It's obvious to him now that he can, and that takes some strain off. He's

pleased about his teaching assignment this year and is getting
into the groove of academic life again. On Wednesday (October 7), I went to class with Andy. Rich has classes on
Wednesday, too, and we get home about the same time,
around 9:00 P.M. When we got home, he asked me if I had
made love to Andy. I told him I hadn't because I wanted to
make love to him before I made love to Andy, since we had
been alienated from each other.

By the end of the week, Rich and I were on our usual
good terms. Sunday started out fine but hit a snag mid-
morning. While fixing his breakfast and in the course of
talking, I happened to mention that sometime I'd like to
show San Francisco to Andy. That hit Rich wrong! Again
it was poor communication. There was another blowup!
Jeez! Amy felt Rich was taking out on her things he felt
bad about with me. He was hurt because I didn't want to
take him or Amy to San Francisco, and I kept saying to
myself, "Why didn't you keep your big mouth shut!" What
I meant and tried to explain was that it wasn't necessarily
Andy I wanted to take to the city and show around; I enjoy
doing that sort of thing (playing tour guide) and did it frequently in Los Angeles. It happens Andy is new and
doesn't know much of San Francisco and would enjoy it.
Also, I assumed Rich and Amy had seen all the sights,
having lived here four years or so.

I needed to get away from the tension building up, so I
took my journal and drove to a lookout point and spent the
entire afternoon writing. By the time I got home (about
6:30), the air was clear, and everyone was in a better mood.
We discussed our feelings at dinner. I apologized to Rich and
tried again (clumsily) to explain what I'd meant. Communicating seems to be the crux. The trick is to say what you
mean *and* what the person spoken to will understand. Mind
reading is impossible and leads to a host of misinterpreta-
tions. I must learn to communicate what I feel, not an easy
thing to do twenty-four hours a day. Still, with our misunder-

standings, we are better off than most. We don't let bad feelings or resentment build up. That's a sure-fire way to poison a relationship. I know that from experience!

School started (again) for Amy on October 5. She's a teaching assistant at Stanford (in addition to teaching the class at San Jose State), which means she's going five days a week now. Her schedule was staggering at first, but she's settling into a routine and beginning to function more smoothly now. She still needs support psychologically, but she is doing fine. It's her fear that keeps her from enjoying teaching, but that too is fading; and I think by semester's end, she'll be comfortable in her role as a teacher. Meanwhile, the hectic pace puts somewhat of a damper on our progress. There simply isn't time for us to get our things together. However, as we all settle into our given routines, we'll take the time and resolve our bisexual feelings.

Sunday, October 18 Last Monday, I went to take my pretest for an encounter group I've enrolled in. Rich thought I would benefit from a T-group, and I'm now attending one which will run for ten weeks.

After taking my test, I went to pick up some bathroom scales, having completely forgotten to get some money. It occurred to me I could stop by Andy's and get my check (he bought my typewriter, and I'd left my check there) and pay for the scales with that. I did stop by and found him studying and horny. We made love, and I left him to his books and took off to finish my errands. As it turned out, no one will accept a second-party check, so I couldn't get the scales. I went on home, and while fixing Rich and me a late lunch, he asked if I had stopped to see Andy, to which I answered yes.

I told him we made love but that I hadn't planned to go see Andy; circumstances contributed to me stopping to see him. Rich seemed more comfortable than he ever had previously about me having made love with Andy. I was concerned and anxious to assure him of my love for him, and we talked at length—and made love.

When Rich knows that Amy or I have made love to someone else, he likes to make love to us when we get home or at the earliest convenient time. It's a kind of restaking his claim, a reassuring act that restates our love and caring and sexual attraction for him. I don't mind—usually. Sometimes it's somewhat of an effort, but the benefits are worth it.

Tuesday is my household-chore day. I grocery shop and clean house. Amy has classes all day, and Rich usually reads or writes. Tuesday evening, I had my first encounter group session. It was very interesting, and I'm looking forward to gaining a great deal from my participation in it. I got home quite late, and we sat up till 2:00 A.M., with me relating all that had happened. One of the men there asked me out, and I gracefully declined, explaining that I was in a group marriage and while I had the freedom to go out, and indeed did go out, I was feeling especially close to my husband and my wife, so, thanks, but no thanks. I was amused at his interested reaction, and expect there will be questions of all sorts. I'm not sure what to expect when the group finds out, as they undoubtedly will somewhere along the line.

Class with Andy on Wednesday, which I find stimulating and interesting, is one of the few times I get to see Andy at all. Aside from the fact that I do enjoy lovemaking with him, I also want to get to know him as a person. I wish I could feel comfortable enough about Rich's reaction so that I could drop by and see him occasionally or we could go to a movie together or whatever. Perhaps that will come.

RICH

Sunday, October 18 Thinking back and leafing through what I have written to this point, I feel a kind of disappointment. It is not enough. It does not penetrate sufficiently. It is neither sharp nor subtle enough. It does not yet go far enough inward, nor does it adequately represent the sociodynamics and interplay of our little group. I feel a desire to go further, further inward and further upward, further in precision of observation and formulation, keener in bringing out significant detail of our lives together.

Perhaps I am only communicating the essence of my mood: depression. For it has been a difficult week for me, with two important highlights. First, I feel much less jealousy toward Andy now. A discussion with Amy last Sunday helped me realize that for a number of reasons, I had not been true to my own principles. Our marriage is a *voluntary* relationship, and it doesn't retain that character if one person is always pressuring another to force his personality into a mold. Neither is it consistent to impose rules on the other which he is not willing to accept voluntarily. It is not fair to demand that the other deny his honest desires and emotions. I have tended to do this with Karen, wanting too much of her for myself, perhaps more than I have yet earned.

The second highlight was my own classes. While I was by no means sharp or well prepared, I *feel* the responses from the students. They do sense my seriousness and enthusiasm, and this is gratifying to me.

We are too serious, too responsible, too heavy. As a result, and because we are so busy, we do not have enough time for one another or enough lighthearted, carefree fun.

I am also encountering some bisexual feelings in myself. As a male, I am less adaptable to such feelings than women seem to be, and I sometimes feel dammed up. Both Karen and Amy are more comfortable with their bisexuality, although they still have difficulty confronting and freely experiencing one another. I sometimes wonder if they ever will.

Amy is loosening up with her classes and finding them less of a chore. I am pleased with this, as I am with Karen's new scholastic interests. She is developing a sense of frustration

as a result of reading about black history and social problems. This is excellent, for it means that her character and
personality, and not merely her intellect, are engaged, stimulated. Also, Amy is finding out, at a higher and more complex level of awareness, what it is to structure and organize
material to make it communicable, digestible, appealing to
the student.

One other thing I am most pleased about is that both Amy
and Karen are taking their journals more seriously. They are
trying to set aside a portion of each Sunday to make an entry
of some sort. Karen brought hers up to date last week and
immediately reacted to her feeling of having clarified some
of her own feelings *to herself.*

Karen's first encounter group session was a success for
her. She came home last Tuesday and related it in fascinating
detail. It will, I am certain now, be beneficial to her.

AMY
Sunday, October 18 Again, a month has passed. It's been
a busy, trying month. The last two Sundays I have tried to
set aside time to write in this journal, but the days were taken
up with stress between us, and when free of it, I sought
diversionary respites rather than the thoughtful immersion
which is necessitated here.

The last month has been difficult, one interpersonal problem after another, complicated by the ever-present and increasing time pressures of our work schedules. We are probably all overcommitted, having each assumed too many
responsibilities.

In a group marriage, down moods spread. That has been
a big problem for us. Rich has been depressed and anxious
a lot in the last month, the continuing depression over his
health and vulnerability which began with his skiing accident
a year and a half ago and has waxed and waned ever since.
He has needed a lot of support from the two of us, and it has

left us drained and oppressed. Under stress, the three of us react differently, and this is a problem. Rich's characteristic response to stress and pressure is an increase in his social needs (a seeking out of people and social support) and an increase in his sex drive. Karen and I both respond to stress by social withdrawal (a seeking of solitude, internal consolidation, and if it is the pressure of work, throwing ourselves into it to bring it under manageable control) and a decrease in our sex drives.

Rich has said that it's seemed like he was reaching out for us and we were slipping further away. Given that we all were under time pressures and have different coping strategies, that's hardly surprising, though Karen and I both tried our best to put our needs aside and respond to him when he reached out. He probably perceived that there was some effort involved in doing so and, at times, a certain resentment as our unmet needs became stronger and stronger. When time is a problem itself, every minute and hour and day given to another increases the pressure on self. We should not have to be so tightly scheduled as we are; we don't have enough time for each other. And all the work makes us all too serious and tired. We are rarely lighthearted, and Karen particularly feels bothered that we hardly ever "have fun together" anymore. To her, that means fooling around or going out to a movie or dinner or something, and I believe she's dissatisfied with us in that way. Yet, she's as likely to read on Friday nights as we are, feeling the pressure of her class assignments. We're all too responsible and too serious, but there doesn't seem to be a way around it without sloughing our job commitments—and that could be disastrous! I have to hold down two jobs so we'll have enough money to live on, but then I don't have much free time or time to play or follow up my other interests. What a dilemma!

It's perfectly understandable to me that when Karen wants to go to San Francisco or go out that she would think of and perhaps prefer going with someone else because we're short on money, we're short on time, and most important, we get so weighted down by work and resolutions of emotional difficulties, it's hard to drop them and just go have fun like on a date with someone else. All of it carries over. Everything has been so *heavy,* and we keep pulling each other down rather than being able to pull each other up. One of us is always tired or depressed or has to work.

KAREN

Sunday, October 25 This week has been full of all kinds of feelings and emotions for the three of us. Rich was depressed and visably upset Monday. Many reasons: An irritating rash drains him of energy, and causes the depression. Then when he's already depressed, he worries about being overweight, his research, the financial situation; and on top of this, he is concerned for and troubled about other people who turn to him for solace and advice. Amy has been upset this week because there simply aren't enough hours in the day. And lately it seems like things have just been caving in on her. I know she feels pushed in preparing for her lectures, but really, since she hasn't had so much time to *worry* about it, she's been doing just great. She comes across more relaxed, and I've really been enjoying the class.

Tuesday, Brian (my ex) called. I don't know exactly why, but it kind of unnerved me. He's getting along fine and seems happy, pleased with school and very fulfilled in his job. He said he'd like to take me out for dinner or drinks soon, and we settled for next Monday, both our schedules permitting. I wonder how I'll feel?

The second session of my encounter group met Tuesday evening. Again, it was a good session and I'm feeling closer to the group. I had a little bit of trouble getting into the feeling of things all evening though; I had one of those damn headaches. Gad, they really put me out of commission. It lasted all day Wednesday, too, and I felt so crummy, I didn't attend Andy's class.

Thursday morning, Rich and I were talking in the kitchen while I prepared lunch. He asked Amy and me where we were in our relationship and where we're going. There was a minor incident which touched off the discussion. It was a rather inopportune time, since Amy is always psyched up on Thursdays for her lecture; so we heard what Rich had to say and promised we'd discuss us on the way home from school, which we did. The conclusion we came to was that part of the difficulty (not just between Amy and me but also among the three of us) is that our schedules aren't flexible enough. We decided we needed to spend some time together, and so we made a date for next Thursday to stop for a couple of drinks on the way home from school. We both feel sexy after a couple of drinks. Neither grass nor LSD make me feel especially sexy.

Speaking of sex, I've been feeling irritable all this week, and the reason finally occurred to me—no sex. My mind knows there have been various reasons (Amy had an infection we want to clear up before we spread it from one of us to the other), but my body doesn't understand. I seem to have difficulty, too, in *asking* Rich to make love to me. Oh, I may do it by teasing or taunting, etcetera, but to come right out and say "Hey—" I can't bring myself to ask. Amy and I discussed this, and it occurred to me that it might partly stem from my experiences with Brian. I could never ask him either. Or perhaps it goes deeper than that. I don't know.

AMY

Sunday, October 25 It's been a good week. Though he still needs to sleep a lot, Rich has been feeling physically better and more intellectually alert and capable. And I have been more relaxed this week about my teaching duties. I have been out of commission sexually this week from my period and a vaginal infection. Karen and Rich haven't been able to get their schedules together for lovemaking either. Three of us living together and no one's made love for over a week—surprising to outsiders, I would imagine, who probably visualize us spending half our time in the sack. Going without lovemaking makes Karen, by her own words, "grouchy and bitchy." We will have to remedy that today and see that it doesn't happen again. After a lapse, she says it's hard for her to have orgasms; even masturbating doesn't work then.

Last night we had our first evening out together for quite a while, and it was good for us. We went to a reception at the home of the only other three-person marriage we know of personally. Sara, Sam, and Jamie got married a year and a half ago in a self-written and self-designed ceremony in a beautiful park (Rich and I attended), and then two weeks ago Sara and Sam (with Jamie as best man) had a formal wedding ceremony back East. Yesterday was their reception for friends here. Afterward, we visited with two other couples at one of their homes. In both places, we found again that being among others socially drew us closer together and increased our awareness of how good the three of us have it together. We feel a strong group identity when in a larger group and revel in our relationship, catering to each other and showing our love—sometimes, it seems, to the amusement and sometimes to the disgust of others. We have heard from close friends that people don't quite know how to deal with us socially as a threesome. An interesting thing happened along those lines a few weeks ago when we had a party here: Three of the five couples who came brought with them another girl and thus came as a threesome! I have no idea whether any of them consciously realized their social modification, but the proportion was so high, it seemed an unlikely chance situation.

RICH

Tuesday, October 27 We have certainly had an on-and-off period recently. Our experiences have run hot and cold, being either very good or very poor. I have been much more up myself, more productive, less depressed, more flexible, less a drain on Amy and Karen.

I foresee more stormy periods as we work to set our marriage on a solid base. This is made difficult by the fact that we all, but especially me, expect so much from the marital relationship. This can be dangerous, placing too many demands on Karen and adding some others to the set of expectations I have of Amy. This might account for some of our interpersonal stress, though most of it is the result of our

rather tight and demanding schedules and our many commitments. Some of those, however, we would not have were
it not for my high level of ambition, my own achievement
orientation, and my refusal (sometimes doctrinaire) to let
any of us turn down opportunities.

However, Amy is beginning to get her classes and her
preparation under control. And Karen is working hard on
her courses, as well as doing my typing, keeping the house
in immaculate shape, and fixing almost all the meals.

We had another experience which brought out further our
emerging identity as a group. We attended a reception on
Friday given by the only other friends we have who are in
a genuine three-adult family (two males, one female). One of
the males and the female were legally married at her home,
I think for the sake of her parents. The other male was the
best man, but they have been living together as three for well
over a year. Our presence at their small reception was definitely as a threesome. We enjoyed the role. Karen got tipsy
on champagne, and we were all in a light mood. I really enjoy
taking them out. I suppose I do like to show them off, but
I try to avoid doing it deliberately and pompously. Besides,
they are each sufficiently attractive to draw plenty of attention without my antics.

Sunday, we were quiet and tired. Karen had been bitchy
for a few days. She had told Amy she wanted to make love
with me but was afraid to ask or approach me, a holdover
from three years of slow and miserable rejection from her
former companion. She was, I sensed, tense and felt strange.
Sunday night, she went to see Andy and had sex with him.
I was not jealous but did feel slighted. My anger was over
Karen's reticence toward me. She was, it seemed, playing a
game, but one she didn't understand herself. I didn't object
to her desire for Andy, but I felt distant from her because she
was unable to express her needs and desires to me.

We had a talk late Sunday night, a very straight and important talk, where I made more plain to her what I expect of her as a person. Perhaps it was what she unconsciously wanted, though she reacted with tears and remorse. She conceded that it was her problem, her problem of being out of touch with herself, unable to express her needs to me, and fearful of a rejection, which she would rarely get from me.

Today, this afternoon after a busy day of typing and cleaning, she walked into the kitchen nude and asked—I had to laugh—for a quickie. Naturally I was pleased. Naturally she got it. I do believe it was one of the very few times in her whole life that she *asked,* directly, for someone to make love to her.

Amy and I and, if I can tell, Amy and Karen are closer, too. As I say, much of it has to do with my health and the subsequent moods it leaves me with. My classes went well on Thursday, and that sets well with me. I love teaching. I take it seriously and enjoy involving myself with students. I am hardly satisfied with either my talent or my status. Still, though, I sometimes feel intellectually lonely, like I can't work a sufficient number of persons into my life. I like to learn from intelligent and sensitive persons, especially women, especially sexy women. Amy is such a woman and strives to satisfy that need in me, but it runs so high that she is sometimes intimidated by it. I guess it's a healthy thing that her charm sometimes distracts me from intellectual pursuits. She tempers me and is learning to effectively criticize me, and I couldn't do my job without her.

I feel good. Life is looking somewhat brighter, especially from the inside, where it counts. I seek new adventures, new ideas, and new personalities. But I think we need to lay our groundwork together more, and more solidly, so that such adventures become not only possible for each of us but are mutually desired for each and for all together. If we achieve that, *then* we will be a real family.

KAREN

Wednesday, October 28 I am very caught up in what happened this last Sunday. We had been abstaining from sex together, and I was getting bitchy, though I understood why. Sunday, I was feeling restless. Amy had some reading to do, and Rich and I were kind of at loose ends. Rich said he didn't know what he wanted to do, so after dinner, I asked Amy if she'd mind if I'd go see Andy for a while. She said no. Rich was in the living room, and I went in and asked him if he minded. He said he felt somewhat slighted and that he'd like my company. I *heard* what he said, and I must have *processed* it. So, I either heard it and ignored it, *or* I heard it, quickly weighed the situation, and decided that *my* needs at that time were such that I very much needed to get out. Anyway, whatever the thought processes were, I did call Andy. It was about 9:30 P.M. He was feeling kind of depressed, so I thought I could get out for a while and at the same time cheer him up. We had a very enjoyable time. I relaxed, and we had some interesting talks—and we made love, although that wasn't the reason I went there.

I got home about 1:30 A.M., and Rich was still up. He was quite upset and said he was tired of putting up with what I was doing. He talked for a long time. I was dumbfounded. He challenged me with things I wasn't *aware* I was doing, or at least I wasn't aware of how they appeared to him. As I later explained to Amy, sometimes I feel as though Rich browbeats me emotionally and puts words in my mouth via his interpretations, which I can't refute. That is, I'm not in touch with that particular thing inside me, and rather than bring up the subject, probe, throw out questions, and help me get in touch with *me,* he interprets and analyzes. Frequently, he's right; in fact, he's *nearly always right,* but on some matters he's blinded by his proximity and emotional involvement. His view of things becomes distorted by his personal feelings.

By the time he was finished, I felt like the condemned, like going out and slitting my wrists. I mean, gad, if I'm all that bad and I'm inflicting *that* much pain, then, hell, this whole thing is a farce, and why am I sticking around? As a favor to him, I should get the hell out of here. It sounded so glum, I wasn't sure if I could ever redeem myself.

RICH

Friday, November 6 Last week was a stormy one with Karen, but it ended on a healthy note, with her and me expressing our feelings and affection very well. After a row, partly my fault, about her relationship with Andy, we straightened things out on Friday after a long and productive discussion. Friday afternoon, we took a wee bit of LSD together and spent the afternoon making love. Later we picked up Amy on campus and returned home, whereupon she joined us. We all had light, uninhibited trips, and we engaged in some very pleasant three-way lovemaking, although Amy could not have intercourse. Both of them let loose and came out to play for a while. They now see the possibility of coming out and being wide open even without the use of chemical agents.

Saturday was quiet but full of good feeling. We spent Halloween watching a series of spook shows on TV, joking, laughing, and generally having a good time.

Karen's encounter group pounced on her charming exterior this Tuesday past. One of the males she had confided in and had been friendly to "betrayed" her, as she put it, by criticizing her for being "too sweet, too happy." She said she nearly cried and was definitely hurt because she had tried to be so open with all of them. She disclosed a great deal about our marriage the week before. Perhaps the men could not stand the deviance, the experimentation, the bisexuality, and other aspects of her interaction with them and so turned on her. She withdrew. But they are having a weekend marathon, and the effect should be beneficial. She realizes the experience is good for her in many ways. I think sooner or later the three of us should get into a group of some sort. There is no particular or crucial reason for doing so except for Karen's inability to fight and manage conflict.

KAREN

Monday, November 9 Thursday before last was school day for Amy and me and the day Rich has his class meet here at home. I was really strung out, partly from lack of sleep and partly from tension and anger. I avoided him, and he me. Amy, who was in the position of middleman, tried to talk about the problem on the way to school, but my anger seemed so final that the discussion went nowhere. School was difficult for me, and I was glad when my last class was over. When we got home, Rich was smiling and obviously pleased that his class had gone well. He tried to kiss me, and I avoided that, too. I went straight to my room and then to bed. I was extremely tired, and my period had begun, so I had cramps, too. He came in and asked if I wasn't even going to talk to him, to which I replied he had already tried and judged and sentenced me, so what was the use. He said good night and left.

Friday morning he came to my room and asked if I wanted to talk. My reply was to pull out my journal and tell him that it's all here. I put it all down on paper at the time I was feeling it. He smiled and said, "I know; I read it yesterday afternoon." I wasn't angry at him having invaded my privacy, as reading my journal without my permission could have been interpreted. Anyway, we got things straightened up—the situation and our feelings. I don't mind admitting that that's something I don't want to go through again!

Friday afternoon, I asked Rich to make love to me. Amy had gone to her class, and I was feeling the need to be close to him after our disagreement. He thought it would be a good idea to take some acid, so we took a small amount and spent the afternoon making love and waiting for Amy to come home to trip, too. About 3:30, we got up to shower. We expected Amy to call us to come pick her up at 4:00 P.M., so we took the phone into the bathroom with us. It got to be 4:00 and then 4:15 and no call, so we began to wonder if she'd gotten delayed somewhere. Suddenly we both remembered at once that we were to pick her up at 4:00. She wasn't *going* to call.

God, well, we left immediately—and wow! It was just beautiful outside. It had rained, and everything looked so clean and fresh. By the time we picked her up, we were forty-five-minutes late; and when she got into the car, it was obvious she was angry. She asked if we had made love, and when we said yes, she said she didn't appreciate being left standing on the street corner while we made love and we should judge our timing better. Rich said "Amy, you're right, but weigh what you're saying. We're both high." We explained the situation and apologized. She accepted the apology, and then we made two quick stops on the way home and spent the evening lightly tripping. We were playful and loving. I got a fantastic breast massage. The three of us were one again. Later we had pizza and watched a movie on TV.

Saturday, we all fussed around the house. Saturday late afternoon, Rich tripped again, and we spent a quiet Saturday night listening to music, watching a movie and eating pizza (again).

Tuesday is my encounter group evening—and brother! What a meeting it was! I had the rug pulled out from under me. I was attacked by people I was coming to trust. It really surprised me; I came home feeling tense and hurt and told Rich and Amy about the meeting. Wednesday I went to class with Andy as usual and came home early. Thursday I got up and got partially ready for school but started to feel nauseated and headachy, so I lay down about 10:30 A.M. I dozed for a while and began to feel worse and worse. Rich wasn't feeling so hot either, so we both decided to take it easy. He canceled his classes, and I went back to bed, and Amy left for school. I felt progressively sick at my stomach and finally deduced I had stomach flu. I couldn't eat and couldn't keep anything in my stomach when I did. By the time Amy got home, I was really feeling crummy. It lasted all night, and Friday morning I felt weak and tired. Amy got up and found someone to substitute for her classes, and since it was rainy and cold outside, we all decided to take the day off. Amy spent most of the day cooking things in the kitchen; I spent the day trying to regain my strength and rest. Rich built us a beautiful fire which we enjoyed all day long. Friday evening at 8:00 P.M., I was to go attend a weekend retreat of my encounter group; it was to last till Sunday afternoon/evening. I was still feeling quite weak and shaky, and yet I *wanted* to attend. I didn't want anyone to think I was copping out because I had been attacked on Tuesday. So I made slow preparations all day to attend, resting in between and not pushing too much.

What a heavy weekend. I felt close to the group and especially close to a couple of people and interested in knowing a couple of others. I have been increasingly impressed with one fellow, David, because of his extremely accurate insights and his nonbullshitting method of dealing with people. He is also *very* tuned-in sexually. He has expressed interest in me from the first. That makes me feel good, and I'm interested in him, though not sexually. That is not to say I will never encounter him that way, but I don't have any particular desire for him sexually. I'd like to get to know him and continue a friendship after the group ends, and I'd like very much for him to meet Rich and Amy. I think he and Rich would stimulate one another. I'm also interested in another fellow, Fred. David is forty-three or forty-four, but I don't know Fred's age. I'd say mid-twenties.

I want to write down the feelings I have now while they're

still fresh in my mind and see how and if they develop and into what, if anything. I felt an attraction to Fred from the first meeting; he has a slightly arrogant way of handling himself that I like. Very confident and somewhat playfully boyish, and at the same time I feel the strong, mature, confident man. I told him in one session he reminded me of my brother and that I liked him. My brother emits this same confident, slightly arrogant air. Anyway, the feelings and attraction grew, and Saturday we felt very close to each other. Coming home from Portola Park Saturday we rode in the back seat with David and Diane in the front seat, and we were feeling very erotically and sensually stimulated. He had his arm around me, and we were holding hands. It was partly (probably a great deal) due to the entire atmosphere of the group. David was in rare form; we were laughing and giggling and being silly and having such fun. We dropped Diane off at her home so she could nurse her baby and went on to David's house.

We had lunch and wine, and people were napping. I spread my sleeping bag on the floor to lie down, and Fred asked if he could join me. We lay there listening to each other breathe and holding hands. He kissed me. I had such beautiful feelings. We just lay on the floor listening to the quiet, and he whispered part of a song—a few lines, one that said something about the silence of our words is meaningful enough, or something like that. It was such a warm, close, stimulating thing. The feelings were very erotic, and yet he made no move toward me that way (clutching or demanding or grabbing), but yet the feelings for both of us were there. It *sounds* paradoxical, but it wasn't.

We both agreed that we felt an overt involvement within the group would perhaps alienate the group or at least set us apart, which we didn't want to happen. By the same token, we didn't deny our attraction and closeness. We discussed our feelings again on Sunday. We were among the last three or four to leave. Fred and I stood out front beside our cars, talking awhile longer. He said he felt very strongly attracted but felt somewhat restrained because of the group. He also said he admired what Rich and Amy and I were into and intellectually understood but didn't know if he could handle it emotionally and to what depth. To sum up our discussion, we decided to adopt a play-it-by-ear tactic.

I came home last night feeling exhausted and exhilarated at the same time. Rich said I was suffering from reentry, and I felt it. It's really a strange sensation. I've been sorting my feelings all day, and I can't grab onto anything concrete. Fred is a different feeling for me, one I can't explain, and it's weird. He isn't handsome, but I find him attractive. He's small, has blue eyes, brown longish hair, and looks very, very young. He's about my height—actually, he's *just* my height —and slight in build. I've been trying all day to put into words or thoughts what my feelings are for him, but perhaps I should instead just put down my feelings or better yet the way he makes me feel: romantic, young, innocent, and very sensuous. I say innocent not to mean excluding sex, only a reintroduction into it perhaps the way I would like it to have been the first time. Tomorrow night the group meets again.

I mentioned to Rich and Amy that what I'd really like to do is have the group *here* sometime. I want Rich and Amy to meet the people I'm talking about. Plus the fact that we have a very comfortable encounter house. I also want them to meet Fred and David in somewhat the same context (the encounter group) in which I know them. Rich and Amy were very open to this.

Monday, November 16 Wednesday I went to class with Andy. He told me he was afraid I'd go to bed with someone during my encounter weekend. He also doesn't want me to become involved with anyone else, and when I told him I was interested in and had become friends with a couple of fellows in my group, he got all bent out of shape. Our relationship seems to have deteriorated for a number of reasons. As I see them, they are that we never get together except for the trip to San Jose on Wednesday or if I stop by to see him. He doesn't seem to be comfortable around Rich and Amy. When we *are* together, I feel a tinge of obligation to make love, since he says I'm the only girl he is seeing. Perhaps all the difficulty I went through with Rich initially had some slight effect, too. Anyway, I am sorry to see the relationship fall apart. Then of course there's the time factor. I simply have to budget my time, especially with the semester drawing to a close and projects due.

Our conversation was a real bummer; I felt as though Andy was giving me the third degree and pushing me to make some decisions about our relationship in a way which only alienated me. Andy was really digging at me and finally became downright vicious. I said that since he felt that way and we obviously misunderstood each other, I didn't care to go to class and started to leave. He asked me to not go, to try to understand he was just hurt. I did go to school with him, and he dropped me off at home afterward. When he walked me up to the door, I invited him in but he declined, even though it was early. He had a really funny uneasy or threatened look cross his face, as though he was someplace he shouldn't be. Perhaps I should be more understanding of those feelings. I wouldn't have handled the whole situation as well if I had been him.

Thursday was filled with classes and Friday with studying and odds and ends. Saturday Fred and I went to San Francisco and just walked around and had a perfectly delightful day and returned to his apartment, where he fixed dinner, and we chatted over wine. We made love, but we didn't have intercourse. I couldn't because of a slight infection. It was so beautiful. We simply lay nude in each others arms, read poetry, and fell asleep.

When I came home, Rich and Amy were up. Rich had gone to Kay's for the afternoon and evening. Rich seemed perfectly at ease about my having spent the day with Fred, and I felt very comfortable that he had made love to Kay. See, we *are* making progress!

By this time, a cold Amy had been fighting had really grabbed hold. It always seems to be first one thing and then another with us. First I had a cold; then Amy had an infection; then our periods; then I had an infection; then I had the stomach flu; now Amy has a cold; and about the time she gets over it, it will be her period again; and a week later, *my* period. It's been so long since *we* made love—too long. I'm beginning to have fantasies about girls again. As soon as all the colds and infections are gone, we're going to put our periods on schedule so that we will have them at the same time and can start a love life together.

RICH

Friday, November 20 As a group, we are stabilizing more and more. As a result, we are becoming able to reach out to others, to extend ourselves further, and seek additional experiences and involvements both as a group and as individuals. Karen's experience with the encounter group is to no small extent responsible for this. It has unlocked some potential for interpersonal experience. She is more confident, to an observable degree, after only a few weeks with it. She has even made romantic contact with one male member of the group and admires and is interested in two or three others, male and female. The effects of this are beneficial at home, with Amy and me. I think we all are finally talking openly and directly about our own erotic relationships. And Karen is better able and feels more free to speak up, to assert herself, her ideas, her opinions about things she does not like. I enjoy observing her as she moves outward from herself, but at the same time more in touch with the inner parts of her own personality. "That's more self-esteem, isn't it?" she said the other day. Indeed it is, if you say so, especially if you believe it when you say so.

Our problem is still that we are overburdened and overextended with work. I am working on the introduction to a book, which Amy proofs and revises and Karen types, and two papers. I am constantly baffled by my ever-widening intellectual interests. I am a victim of the information explosion as well as being exploited to some extent by being bought as a cheap teacher via teaching assistantships. Amy is constantly busy, but she, too, is finding herself as a teacher and intellectual. We all find ourselves complaining about too much work, too heavy schedules, not enough free times for our personal pursuits and interpersonal explorations. At least one of us is working every day, including Saturdays, Sundays, and holidays. I convinced Amy to call off her lecture class, which would give her a substantial break along with Thanksgiving and next weekend. She is not physically strong or durable, and it often takes two to three weeks for her to recover from a simple cold that should be over in two or three days.

AMY

Sunday, November 22 We seem to have entered a new phase in our relationship together. I have a feeling of having passed through three other phases or stages. Let's see if I can summarize them: The *first phase* was one of newness, which began on July 4 when Karen joined us in the Rockies. It continued for a number of weeks, perhaps until mid-August when we returned home from the extended camping trip to Baja and Stanislaus, and was characterized by getting to know each other, sharing the details and particulars of our personal histories, and learning each others' moods, habits, mannerisms, strengths, and weaknesses. We each had a picture of the other, but it wasn't filled out.

The *second phase* began when we each realized—at about the same time, I think—that we had begun to feel at home with each other and together. It was the dawning and awareness of a distinctly different feeling. Where we lived felt now like our home, the home of the three of us, with Karen a new full-fledged member. The return from the camping trip most likely precipitated these feelings and was responsible for them occurring in each of us at roughly the same time. As this period continued, we basked in the new feeling and settled in together, feeling more comfortable letting our hair down with each other—not *always* being fixed up (dressed and "manicured"), not so concerned with and conscious of how we were being perceived but more relaxed in just being ourselves, and occasionally (though not often) not closing the bathroom door.

That latter has been a funny aspect of growing intimacy. In a joking way, Rich has tried to desensitize Karen on that. Once she came into the bathroom while he was in the tub and once while he was in the shower and had asked him how soon he'd be through because she had to go to make shi-shi. Each time, he's tried to get her to go ahead and go! It's always been a humorous situation, sometimes with me ganging up and making it more hilarious by crowding into the bathroom with them. A few weeks ago, Karen told Rich she closes the bathroom door now because *I* do! I think I picked it up from her! Rich and I had always done as convenience dictated. If we were in the middle of a conversation, we'd leave it open or both walk in there still talking.

The *third phase* was a stormy one, characterized by ups and downs, mostly downs. Just when I'd get things stabilized, Rich and Karen would get into another fight. I was partially removed during this period, feeling the pressure of my work, as the teaching schedules started, and tending to my academic commitments. I felt overburdened with work and often exasperated at the extra strains Rich and Karen were putting on me by *their* interpersonal difficulties, mostly touched off by their jealousies and insecurities about their respective relationships with others. At the same time, they were each in their own ways trying to bolster and support me in the new challenges I faced with teaching, and I don't know what I would have done without both of them, for they each were capable of giving me different kinds of support which I needed.

During this period, there were a few times when I thought we weren't going to make it, when we seemed to me very close to breaking up, though I may have taken things too seriously, being the one who was least directly involved in the troubles and therefore least able to take steps toward resolution. One such occasion when Karen thought rather seriously, it seemed to me, about leaving was the day after the party we had here when she cut out and left without saying anything and went to Andy's.

I'm not sure when this period of instability and violent up-and-down swings reached its end, but it seems to have. I'm not sure how to characterize this new phase yet, but the stormy period I think has passed.

We're all closer than ever before. One thing which has definitely contributed to that is Karen's experience of being in an encounter group. She joined it in the beginning of October at our suggestion, and it won't be over until the middle of December. She was really cute when she came home from her encounter group one time and told us they had told her she was "too straight," in the way she dressed and looked primarily. She now feels motivated to do something about that because she doesn't want to be that way. It's humorous to me that this occurred sometime *after* she had told them about her group marriage and bisexuality. They were, of course, responding to a different aspect of her, but the juxtaposition has its amusing qualities! Between the encounter group and the two LSD trips the three of us have taken together, she has learned more what it's like to relate truly openly, to know herself better and be open to realizing how she really feels, why she says and does things. She is now more conscious of her own defenses when threatened and even calls herself on them at times, as well as responding with less evasion when we call her on them. She is not constantly open in those ways. None of us are, although Rich approximates it the most. But she is aware of what it's like to be closed up and that most people are and what it's like to be open, something which she wants to be more of the time.

That helps the three of us because she can now see what it is we've been wanting from her. Before, she was confused, not understanding why she kept disappointing us. She was giving all she knew how to give but sensed it wasn't enough and felt hopelessly inadequate at times. We have been too hard on her sometimes in that way. But now she is able to pin down what it is we want from her and know that she wants it, too, and it's just a matter of learning *how*.

I have struggled with learning how for a long time myself, fighting hard as Rich tried to draw me out and see into me, to make me look at myself even after I knew I wanted it, too. When these defenses are up, you're caught inside yourself without even being aware at the time that you're not being the way you want to be. But Karen learns fast and has come a long way very quickly. She came out on her first acid trip; whereas for several, I fought and struggled as I felt my defenses stripped away and my vulnerable real self exposed. Even though I had always felt and told myself, *meaning* it, that I could face anything I found in myself and in fact would want such knowledge, I must have been insecure, afraid for a long time (until last spring) to acknowledge to myself and others just how afraid of other people I really am. Since that time, my personal self-confidence has at last been able to increase, and I am more often out than in now, though not out *all* the time, as I had felt maybe was finally true earlier in these pages.

Rich and I haven't had intercourse for over a month! He and Karen have both been in and out of commission. This is all due to a gonorrhea scare, a communicable vaginitis infection, the common cold, twenty-four-hour flu, and a mysterious discharge which Karen now has. As soon as my present period and my present cold are over, I'm going to tackle them both, separately and together. I *think* and hope Karen and I are about ready to make some progress and mainly need to develop some facility both in approaching each other and in making love to each other.

She even mentioned a couple of days ago we're going to have to do something about our periods. They currently occur one after the other, so for two out of every four weeks roughly, one or the other of us is at least partially out of commission, whether heterosexually or homosexually. I have been thinking that if the women in a group marriage have their periods at the same time, it would be to their advantage as far as sex between them and would be no heterosexual disadvantage for either. It would also be better for group sex, in that all could be full participants more of the time. Karen's suggestion that we arrange ours to occur at the same time, something I have been wanting to rearrange myself, strikes me as a move in a positive direction in terms of our sexual relationship, especially since I had previously figured out the above. She said she had begun fantasying about other girls, and I have been too, as well as about Karen, for quite some time now, but then I think I have more of a bisexual desire than she does or at least desire her more than she does me. We shall see.

Both Karen and Rich have new romantic and sexual interests outside the family just now, and I feel a bit left out and resentful that I don't also. Particularly so because there's a guy I'm very much attracted to who, it seems, does not feel the same strong warmth and sexual awareness for me in return. What an upsetting situation. In the past when I have felt a really strong pull or attraction for someone, it has been decidedly mutual, and I had come to assume that when I had a feeling of such intensity toward another, I could count on it being a two-way thing. Well, this time it wasn't, and that is very disappointing. The idea came up recently of having a party of just the three of us and our dates sometime, and it was an amusingly novel idea to imagine. That might be fun sometime, but my first reaction was, "But *I* don't have anyone to invite!"

Tuesday, November 24 Karen's encounter group came over tonight en masse for coffee and wine after their evening session ended. It had pleased me that she wanted to have them over to our home and to share them with us and us with them. She had fussed over having things ready for them— a little too much so from Rich's point of view. He felt that there was something incongruous about formality toward one's encounter group, which in many ways can be considered to have as its end getting underneath and behind that sort of thing. I don't think she had made that connection. Perhaps her behavior was indicative of some insecurity on her part. She had so wanted it to go well, and it did. They were a nice group, and after having already spent several hours together in the group tonight before coming here, conversation and socializing were instantaneous on arrival. I think Rich may have come on a bit strongly and aggressively, but that's his way of displaying interest and being social upon initial acquaintance. He is not one to be without something to say. I felt quite comfortable initiating and being absorbed into conversations. It can be difficult to interact immediately after an encounter session with others who have not just been through the experience, so I was concerned to minimize any such abrasive, gear-changing quality in our meeting and was able to do so effectively, bypassing standard get-acquainted trivia. Karen seemed happy with the evening.

It was touch-and-go earlier this evening between Rich and me. He was feeling restless from having been in the house all day and feeling rather down lately fighting his fatigue, which necessitates a frustrating work slowdown. Our different schedules sometimes contribute to such conflict. Karen and Rich are around the house most days and thus get restless at times; whereas almost every day I have outside commitments on campus and am ready to slow down and relax when I'm at home or pile into more work that has to be done.

Today I left at 9:00 A.M. and had taught three classes, getting home at 3:00 P.M. I was ready to relax quietly for the rest of the afternoon and evening, so our moods were quite different. Rich was feeling "sexually, socially, and intellectually frustrated," and I spent the greater part of the afternoon and evening trying to help him cope with those feelings.

The more deviant we become—the more educated and intellectually developed, the more sexually liberal, and the more open and in touch with ourselves—the fewer people there are capable of becoming close friends. Perhaps this is because we are looking for so much in our social relationships. There is a certain loneliness, social loneliness, that results. Being more of an extrovert and socially oriented than I, Rich feels it all the more strongly, and I don't quite know how to help resolve it for him and indeed for all of us. Lowering our standards or desires would not be satisfying, but finding and getting to know the kind of people we would like to know is a real problem. In our near desperation, we have currently placed an ad in an underground paper. If only one good friendship results, this move will be judged a success, however unlikely or weird such a route to making friends may sound. What a strange society! So "civilized" that we all live in our own little boxes shut off from the others around us, and all of us in our own ways lonely!

Rich's sexual frustration is in part a function of our various physical ailments of the past month. But it is also due to his developing bisexuality, which he has had no real chance to explore except through fantasy and shared imagination with me primarily and with Karen. Nowhere near as many men are exploring bisexuality as women, and thus he has difficulty—an impasse, to date—finding a male friend to actually explore physical intimacy with. I have not been able to be much help to him in finding such a person, and I think he feels a certain resentment about that, since he was actively concerned to support me and help me find opportunities to explore when I was first developing *my* bisexual feelings. I have always met far fewer sensitive, attractive, personable guys than Rich has met such girls, and now he is ever so much more aware of that situation. He doesn't want just an exploitative, experimental sexual relationship with another guy, but rather a sincere intellectual, social, and sexual friendship, and that's just not easy to come by. I hope we will be able to work this out before long, so that he can move out of the realm of fantasy and into determination of his feelings, resolution, and concrete acceptance. He is currently fixated at the fantasy stage and has been for several months, and I don't think this is healthy.

Thursday, November 26 We had a delicious Thanksgiving dinner today, but socially the occasion left something to be desired. Our only guest was a guy from Karen's encounter group whom she has been seeing on a romantic basis outside the group. He's very comfortable to be with and interesting to talk with, so I had anticipated he would be good company today and that the four of us would have a pleasant, relaxed time together. I suppose I should have known better. There's a tendency for pairing off to occur in a four-person group, and what with Karen's and Fred's romantic interest in each other, that pretty much characterized the day. That's all well and good and perfectly understandable but effectively meant that Karen had a date for the day. And Rich and I, who had wanted to share the day and enjoy the company of others, did not have any such company. Rich especially had been feeling socially lonely and deprived and had suggested inviting other friends to join us for dinner and the day, but Karen had been opposed to any other invitations suggested, so we didn't extend them. Sometimes I feel she is selfish in that way, though I don't think she means to be. As I have mentioned, it is difficult to find people whom all *three* of us like. In a very simple statistical sense, one can see that it's bound to be that way. There is practically no one as yet whom all three of us like and enjoy in a roughly equal sense and whose company we seek as a group. There was one such couple,

Kathy and Bob, and we all had a marvelous time together; but since they moved to New England there has really been no one. We're going to have to find a way to correct this situation, for it keeps cropping up and causing disturbances. It's now midnight; Rich has just gone to bed, and I am going to join him. Karen and Fred are still in the living room as a twosome. All of us are left with some unresolved alienation feelings, as Rich and I each expressed our feeling to Karen earlier this evening when she inquired if everything was all right, detecting of course that it was not. Another couple joined us at my invitation for the latter part of the evening and helped to salvage the social frustration of the day. Even in the larger group, Karen and Fred paired off and sat back from the rest of us, conversing. If Karen had her way, the other couple wouldn't have come over at all.

I'm obviously disturbed by the situation, to be carrying on at such lengths about it here. Three is just not a natural unit in our society, and we keep falling back into the normative patterns of pairs despite ourselves. When the day comes that we don't, we will have truly established a group identity and group marriage, but not until then.

KAREN

Friday, November 27 It's Thanksgiving vacation and a welcome rest from daily schedules.

My encounter group the Tuesday before last was really a good one. After the meeting, Susie and I stopped at Fred's for coffee. We had a delightful time. I got home about 2:30 A.M., and who should I find sitting in front of my house but Andy. I sat out front and talked to him for about forty-five minutes. I really feel as though I'm easing him out and he feels it, too, but *I don't want to.* Partially it's the time factor. I don't know what to do about it.

Luann had called from Dallas on Thursday while I was at school and talked to Amy. She's having all sorts of difficulty in her relationship with Alma. So on Friday I called her and tried to encourage and advise her, but that's difficult to do effectively by phone.

On Sunday Fred and I went to the new art museum. We had a fun day people watching and then came home and had dinner here. Tuesday last we had a beautiful encounter group, and everyone came here afterward. A few people stayed late; Fred was the last to leave. We were having a good discussion and feeling very sexy toward one another, though we didn't make love.

I went to class with Andy as usual on Wednesday, but it was the day before Thanksgiving, and no one showed up for class, so we sat around for forty-five minutes to an hour playing the piano and talking. When I came in, Rich was lying down, so I flopped on the bed beside him because I had a tummy ache and cramps. Amy joined us, and she and Rich made love. I felt like I wanted to let the two of them enjoy their lovemaking alone, since it had been so long since Amy had had sex. But I felt awkward about leaving, so I just enjoyed watching them enjoy. I went off afterward to get the clothes out of the washer. Apparently Rich thought I was frustrated and downstairs masturbating. (I wasn't.) After expressing this concern to Amy, he came to my room, and we chatted awhile. Amy is still run down both physically and mentally from the cold, school pressures, lack of sex, and more. She had smoked some pot, and as she walked out of the bedroom, Rich caught an expression on her face and asked what was wrong. He forced her to let out her feelings. She was upset because of the worries he sometimes unnecessarily lays on her, especially about his relationship to me.

As a secondary problem, Amy was feeling that I was preventing her from deepening her relationship with Joyce. Amy had felt inhibited (because of *my* feelings about Joyce) about asking her over, too.

Rich and Amy had another disagreement about her smoking cigarettes, and they were both upset. I spoke with him and agreed that Amy shouldn't smoke and that she should improve her eating habits, *but* I feel Rich's timing is frequently off. He challenges her when she is psyched up for her class or when she is feeling especially run down and in need of relaxation. This unnerves her.

Things were finally resolved, and then came Thanksgiving Day, with lots of good food! Fred came over and read me *Winnie-the-Pooh* stories while I fixed the turkey. The dinner was good, but the day was strange. Fred and I took a walk down to the park and chatted. One part of our conversation centered around the day and how it had turned out. Fred said he felt comfortable in our home but not especially wanted. That is, Rich and Amy tolerate (that's actually a stronger term than I want to use) him because of me; they don't especially like him because of him. I said I understood and that I felt the same way. I also confessed that there are other situations in which I do the same thing with friends of theirs whom I don't especially care for. Soon after we came home, Joyce and her date, Dan, arrived, so we all sat and chatted for quite some time. After about an hour, I began to feel those same frustrating feelings about being trapped in a social situation and not being able to get out of it. I was bored and restless and would much have preferred to be in the kitchen making chocolate-covered nuts.

Friday I was up early and putting dishes away in the kitchen when Rich wandered out. About that time, Fred called and invited me to dinner on Saturday night. I said I didn't know what we had planned and I'd call him back. I asked Rich what, if anything, did we have planned, and he brought me up to date on the subject of Joyce and Amy's feelings.

The crux is, of course, Amy's and my bisexuality. Rich called a meeting and presented his thoughts, insights, and predictions to us. Amy and I have been drifting further apart, and a good deal of the responsibility falls onto our feelings of sexuality toward each other and the frustration of nothing happening. We both feel shy and clumsy and have a tendency to let other things (chores, school, etcetera) take precedence over our working out these things between us. We had a very standoffish discussion. We did agree with him that something needed to be done and it had better be soon. He and I seem to get more easily involved with people more quickly and on a more intimate level than Amy does. She finds so few people who meet her expectations, and it is frustrating to me and must be ten times more so for her that I can't seem to get my head straight about Joyce. Amy is beginning to feel somewhat intimidated that Rich and I have outside interests and the one person she is interested in sexually and socially, I have difficulty dealing with. This puts her in the predicament of not wanting to hurt me but of also not wanting to have to limit her friendships.

Our discussion ended unresolved, and Rich went to his study to read. Amy said, "I love you, Karen," which always melts me totally. I couldn't possibly have accomplished anything here, so I went to the library and finished reading a book for school. I stopped by Fred's on the way home to tell him I couldn't join him Saturday for dinner. He's so very understanding and "there."

When I came home, things were better, but the tensions weren't gone. At dinner Amy asked if she could have the pleasure of my company for the evening, to which I replied, YES!

Rich went to Abe and Maggie's, and Amy and I lay in front of the fireplace talking. We really opened the channels of communication and discussed frankly a lot we had been avoiding. I love her so much and truly desire her sexually, but I'm so shy about conveying these feelings to her. We realized how very much we rely on Rich as a go-between and decided we both want to be able to deal and interact with one another directly. We discussed our sexual shyness and the fact that each of us has trouble believing that the other finds us sexy. The main discovery we made is that Amy makes no demands on me and I make very few on her. That covers a heck of a lot of territory. Since she never makes demands on me or never expresses negative feelings, I have come to assume that whatever I do is all right with her, that it's *Rich* I have to be concerned with. For instance, I never expect her to say, "Gee, I would rather you didn't go out this weekend so we can spend it together." She never has, and she has been so supportive to me when I was going through the Andy thing with Rich. She's just so great, and I really feel lucky to have her, but somehow I'm not able to reciprocate.

I suggested that Amy plan to see Joyce tonight (Saturday). I felt that perhaps a process of desensitization is necessary and would be helpful to me in coping with my feelings about Joyce and about Amy spending time with someone else, a process I've gone through with Rich but not with Amy. I didn't have intentions of playing the martyr, but I think I see the greater long-term benefits of my freeing Amy's mind of guilt and my having to deal with a problem that's in *my* head.

We spent such a delightful quiet evening lying in each other's arms, and we both began feeling sexy, but, alas, it was my period. We had begun to make love when Rich returned home. But all was not lost. Amy took a rain check—redeemable at any time!

KAREN

Monday, November 30 On Saturday Joyce had out-of-town guests, so we decided to trip. We really all had a heavy interpersonal thing. We took the acid about 5:00 P.M. and didn't get to bed until 6:00 A.M.

Rich poured out his feelings, resentments, and frustrations about Amy and I and our not being able to get things together between us and his fears of what this may lead to. She and I had come to some conclusions and had started on the way to becoming closer on Friday night, but we worked on it even more on Saturday.

Rich said Amy and I are inhibiting him socially, and he isn't able to work as he would like to, that one of the reasons he had put the ad in the underground paper was to find the three of us new playmates and new friends as a group. That isn't to say we shouldn't each have friends of our own, but as a threesome we need new friends. *But,* he said, he wanted to do that with the feeling that everything is groovy among the three of us, not to turn to others because he needs outside stimulation he *should* and could be getting here if Amy and I would shape up. In my head, I still have fears that I can't be what I know I have the potential for. That's frustrating as hell.

I had some strange hallucinations. The woman in the picture over the fireplace kept changing with each beat of the music. At first I was just amused. Then I began to see her as me, and me as every woman. I was so many things; the painting even became a man, and that was me, too. The painting didn't scare me, but the implications of my seeing did. I guess such fear is rooted in low self-esteem. The whole thing is paradoxical. I am all those things, warm and beautiful and female and masculine and firm and smiling and cool and on and on. And I really *know* I am, but I don't always want to admit it. Why? Why do I try to ignore all the bad parts? Why do I ever perceive some as bad?

I suggested that we take more trips, but with one of us straight to sort of facilitate between the other two. I know I have some things I'd just like to work out in my head, but I need help. I'd also like to trip with Rich while Amy facilitates and with Amy while Rich facilitates. I'd be willing to facilitate between them, though I feel they don't need it. Perhaps that's a wrong assumption on my part. When the three of us are high, it's difficult to interact. I don't know if Rich and Amy feel this or not, and perhaps I will eventually reach a point where it will be easier to stick to us, rather than just go into myself.

Amy was put on the spot about her body. She needs to take better care of it. On the outside it looks fine (I find her body a real turn-on), but she has got to be nutritionally deficient because of the food she eats. Cokes and potato chips are her chief fare. She asked Rich to please show more attention to foreplay when making love, and he said part of the reason she isn't "ready" is because of a decreased libido and this is caused by not giving her body the proper fuel. I think he is correct, but I also think she has the right to ask for more foreplay. I think this is an area where I can play an important part also, and I intend to.

Rich suggested we check about getting into an encounter group that is somewhat sexually oriented, like the one Kay suggested. I feel like balking at that because I always shy away from sharing problems with outsiders, be they friends (especially friends) or whatever. However, I think the suggestion is a good one, and I'm willing to try it for that reason. I really value the group I'm in now. A situation in which we three interact not only with each other but also with others might be good for us.

We all slept late on Sunday and still were exhausted when we got up. Our trip had taken a lot out of us. Amy and I had made a date for Sunday evening, and we sort of did nothing much all afternoon. Rich was rather standoffish. I had the feeling he had laid something on us and now was standing back, hands on hips, waiting to see some results. Amy felt this, too. We discussed it at dinner, and he said, yes, he felt that way and that he was tired. After dinner he asked for a massage, and Amy and I obliged him. We spent the rest of the early evening trying to implement some of what we'd discussed. It was somewhat strained and tense. Amy and I felt pressured to perform. We (the three of us) did make love, and Amy and I are feeling more comfortable, I believe. One of my hang-ups is that she looks so fragile that I'm afraid I'll hurt her. She assured me that after eight years with Rich, she is quite unbreakable! Now it's up to me to get that notion out of my head and stop inhibiting or repressing some of my pent-up lusty playfulness.

AMY

Monday, December 7 Friday night we had the leader of Karen's encounter group and her husband over. Karen was socially uptight all evening. Saturday she said she was too tired and didn't want to go to the party the three of us had planned to attend. Rich challenged her, and her defenses rose sky-high. Rich and I went to the party, and Saturday and Sunday were characterized by social distance and relative lack of communication around here.

Karen is feeling the pressure of term projects due at school, especially that of an hour oral presentation she has to make in two weeks. She vomited from nerves over the latter last night, and she is worn down and fatigued by the pressure combined with fear. How our various insecurities eat up our energy! Uptightness is tiring.

She and I made candles for Christmas presents on Saturday and Sunday, but it wasn't anywhere near as much fun as it could have been. It's discouraging that whenever I plan to take a day off and just relax and enjoy some creative project of leisure, some damned interpersonal problem arises. When breaks from a heavy schedule are rare, they are all the more cherished—and all the more disappointing when lost.

We've taken two recent acid trips together. The first was on the Saturday after Thanksgiving and was an interpersonally powerful one. In the beginning, I had a bit of a fight with my insecurities, characterized by difficulty in relinquishing my censor mechanism, which would leave me bare and defenseless in front of Karen, who was flitting around the room like a child engrossed in baubles, gurgling in delight but by no means interpersonally open. She was so cute—nude and clutching a thick sheepskin rug like Linus's blanket and looking every bit like Little Annie Fannie from *Playboy,* complete with wondrously big eyes, all rounded, and even the knees-together, toes-turned-in innocent stance. She struck me as a toy, an empty-headed sexual powder puff. Ooh, how she would be *enraged* at that conception! Her encounter group applied that term to her once, much to her resentment; but it does seem apt at times, even though I know there is much more to her.

From that state of childlike ultrafemininity, she progressed to a real awareness and recognition of a masculine component of her personality by focusing on a painting of a woman hanging above our fireplace. The woman kept changing as she looked at her and became a man. Karen was very emotionally involved in the experience and had to struggle not to shut it out and turn away from the picture. These masculine identity feelings have come out before, especially on our first acid trip together, where she was competitive with Rich.

I truly believe everyone has both masculine and feminine feelings, as they are defined for us socially; and as we are channeled at an early age into gender-appropriate behavior, we feel a need to deny and effectively suppress our complementary characteristics. It occurred to us on the trip that Karen's ultrafemininity may well be a compensation for perhaps rather strong masculine feelings which she has been socialized to feel as threatening to her self-image and must therefore deny.

Once during the trip, we reached what seemed to me a very bleak point which made me doubtful about our future as a group. But Karen accepted the challenge and instead of giving up suggested that we needed many more acid trips and that perhaps we would get farther if instead of all of us turning-on at the same time, two of us took acid and the third served as a facilitator.

RICH

Tuesday, December 8 A lot has happened in these past two to three weeks: the tense and aloof Thanksgiving Day, the trauma and conflict of the LSD trip, the difficulties getting in touch with each other. The acid trip in particular was a peak and a valley emotionally and served to elicit some latent responses and bring things to consciousness that needed to be there so that we may collectively cope with them.

Karen surprised me toward the end of what had been a stormy and for me somewhat disappointing, but by no means wasted, trip by suggesting that we turn on more often in different combinations in order to find each other. She now recognizes and respects the power of LSD, properly handled, to produce insight and growth. It has shown her things she didn't know about herself.

On that trip, Amy and Karen became aware of the emotional distance between them. Karen's masculine feelings emerged again, though this time she recognized them. And I—I acted as guide and facilitator, somewhat by default I should say, and didn't get very far into myself, music, or intellectual themes, my usual fare.

The trip left a strain, but each of us was pleased to finally drag out some covered emotions. I am now recognizing my own bisexual feelings more explicitly and comfortably and now feel, after some time, open for experiences with men. I doubt greatly that I am a homosexual, and I also doubt the likelihood of finding acceptable males. But in any case, I feel like one more important taboo—along with religion, conventional marriage, financial orientation, and several others—is resolved. Our culture cheats us that way. Ours is probably the most repressed culture in history, Puritan England included. Certainly so in comparison to the relative level of opportunity for personal development, intellectual exploration, and the pursuit of a good, healthy, examined life. I feel no less masculine. I do feel more expanded, more sensitive, more secure, more aware.

We live in a world of false gods. All the things we are traditionally taught to revere are sham. Money, monogamy, prestige, status, custom, power. Karen often wonders why I am so disdainful of rules. There are two brief answers. One is that they were made by those living in either other times or other places with other ideas and other purposes.

The second, far more significant answer is simply that the rules were made by someone else. I value making my own rules. It's a terrifying and horribly difficult task, but any other kind of ethic in life is a compromise. We must, of course, compromise in general ways in order to exist with our fellows. But far too much is a matter of perceiving the other in order to act accordingly. What we fail to see is him perceiving us, trying to do the same thing. A true comedy of projections. And all, not for the sake of the common good, a humanistic end, a communal purpose, but rather for the individual end of making it, being accepted, joining in order to avoid being responsible for one's own deeds and decisions.

I prefer to make my own rules—because as Socrates contends—if you fail to do so, you will be ruled by inferiors and made subject to inferior rules. The effects are surprising when I try to take this advice out of the public context for which it was intended and apply it to the realm of interpersonal relations.

I suppose some of my difficulties with Amy and Karen are a result of waiting for them to recognize, appreciate, and catch up with the above. Since not many persons of my acquaintance live this way, not even as many intellectuals as I had hoped (their superior intellect makes them the worse sinners in my eyes), I am often lonely. This is not vain romanticism about the significance of the universe or the origin of ethics in the human species—nothing so heavy or abstruse—but rather a practical consequence of living out a deviant style of life. Despite the loneliness, I wouldn't trade it for a home with a pool in the suburbs, a membership in the country club, and a quarter-of-a-million-dollar life insurance policy. I don't think I'll even trade it for tenure at a good university if authenticity, growth, and autonomy are the price.

I prefer to make my own rules. Therefore, I am dangerous. Not violent, not even militant, hardly a loud protester. Just dangerous because I strike at the presumed foundations of social life. I do not own a gun. I do not want to own a gun. I believe in the power of ideas, books, theories, concepts, ideals to influence men's *and* women's behavior. But I and my type are dangerous. To subvert with a sentence, that is my weapon. To alter mood with a word. To transcend a limitation by pointing it out. To teach. That is, after all, my vocation.

AMY

Thursday, December 10 Just this minute I finished reading Philip Wylie's novel *Disappearance,* and I feel overwhelmed, softened, at peace, expanded. Tranquillity above the pettiness, the fears and insecurities, the truly trivial concerns which occupy so much of our daily thought. We become lost in our busyness, in the trees unaware of the forests, focused intently on things which do not deserve it, avoiding and missing that which does, lost in our own excesses, which serve to protect us from what we fear we cannot handle or face, passing our time in a protective coating which shields us even from the knowledge of our waste, imbuing small things with importance, and rarely finding the time to devote ourselves to the things that really matter.

How to know when we deceive ourselves and when we do not? On acid you can tell—I think! Acid, as we use it, shows up our usual defenses, once you discover the language of defenses, once you become aware of your mind in its process of blocking things out—the clouding up of consciousness when another part of your mind senses a threat, for example. When you pass through your insecurities on acid (and without, though perhaps not with such a brilliance), your mind feels sharp and unclouded, and you feel straighter than straight. Your mind and the world about you seem clearer than they ever have, a crystal-clear, diamondlike brilliance. You are aware of so many levels of communication. When someone says something to you, you get an immediate sense of perhaps twelve different levels of meaning that they are communicating, all of which are accurate perceptions, none inconsistent, just representing different levels. We all experience this in a lesser form when we catch an overtone and distinguish between what was said and what was also meant but not said or when we feel a rapport, a very special rapport, with someone and know what they are feeling and what more they are meaning than they actually said. Sometimes we can confirm our accuracy with the person later, reveling and delighting in the intimacy of the experience. But when you perceive several different levels of meaning, it is often hard to know on which level the person is communicating intentionally and which level to respond to. By the level we choose to respond on, we display our trust or distrust of the other, our security or insecurity. To respond on a level different from that which the other person intended is to take the risk of being tuned out, warded off, defended against. If you are insecure, such a defensive response from the other will make you feel uncomfortable and overextended, and you will back off; if you are secure, such a response at times will be mildly amusing, a bit disappointing probably. If you are secure, you may refuse to be rebuffed, resist the defense either by calling the person on it or by ignoring the defense and responding to what's behind it, trying again to get the other to come out of his shell. Or you may decide that the person needs his defense and to let him keep it for now, or decide that it's not worth the effort.

I had been noticing, for a few days before I made this last entry, a change in my overall feeling. I was aware of feeling much more composed than I had for some time, a feeling of a calm amid work and commitments instead of feeling over-run by all I have to keep in order and accomplish. So often this fall I have felt strung out and hassled by my work load, but a strange and satisfying sense of calm has pervaded the last few days. I have gotten much more done with much less strain. I have a feeling it started as I got into Wylie's novel.

As a result of my feelings and reflections on completing the book, I decided I wanted to take an acid trip and consider the nature of my own reality. With that intention, Rich and I took some together, while Karen fooled with other things like making candles. Together we had an exhilarating intel-lectual trip, which centered around some theory construc-tion of a large-scale nature that Rich has been doing. We went to his study to pin down a few points and so he could read to me passages juxtaposed from several theorists. Never before had I understood the full meaning of the words he read to me. At the time and since, it is hard for me to grasp the complexity of meaning, but the import of the implica-tions was clear and overwhelming. Rich's "playtoys" are so much bigger than mine! I have never played with basic con-cepts and paradigms, but his mind is at home with such things, and I was able to see for really the first time in a concrete sense the nature of his mental toys. I stand in awe. He took me with him to what was like a new world of mental functioning, not one created by acid, but one I could share and experience with the aid of acid. What he shared with me was what he had been working on for quite some time when *not* under the influence of acid. I kept getting a visual picture of I-beams, girders joined in an uncompleted structure sus-pended in space. Like being above the lights of the city at night with this structure composed of girders suspended in space, and he was sitting on one of the girders, and I was sitting as a visitor, a privileged guest and companion, on another. The structure was his plaything, like that of a cosmic child, and the girders were visual representations of concepts which together formed an uncompleted and developing theory. My god, it was exciting!

When we had gone to his study, I had been impressed, upon entering, with its similarity to an energy cell. With the flick of one wall switch, the room began to come to life. The lights came on; the two electric heaters started to hum and glow and radiate warmth. The room was walled with books, and two tape recorders sat ready to retain the verbal word. Rich as the central power source had made an energy cell to nourish and extend his mind. When he is well and functioning, he is very much like a power cell—a ball of seemingly self-sustained energy it's hard to keep up with. During the last two years, since the accident, he has been drained; and I have often had more energy than he did, something which had never occurred prior to the accident. The comparison is very clear, now that we have come out the other side and he has again begun functioning at his old level at times.

RICH

Thursday, December 24 Amy and I returned night before last from a pleasant and somewhat refreshing four-day visit with her mother at a ranch in southern California. Amy and I enjoyed the scenery and riding, but the company at the ranch was stiff, and an atmosphere of pseudoinformality pervaded the place, which was said to cater to the exhausted executive. The return to Karen, home, Palo Alto, and work was gratifying. We were urged to stay through Christmas, but it was obvious that we did not belong. The straight world, especially the straight business world, is boring, laced with ennui to the point of madness even in its more restful spots. Amy and I spent the evenings talking while the others drank and played cards, a dreary combination if ever there was one. Meal conversation was dreadful, with many unfeeling and uninformed references to the "black problem," "student unrest," and "high prices." How I long for good company, sensitive interaction.

Last week was very hectic and tiring for us all but produced little or no conflict. Perhaps we were so busy and preoccupied that we had no time for it, but I think it was rather a healthy sign. Cooperation and capable functioning under pressure are signs of harmony. Karen's paper, about which she was very worried, went well, and that was a real boost to her. She becomes more confident with each step she takes. Naturally I am pleased and proud of her. Amy had many papers to grade as well as classes to meet and performed admirably, even though it cost her much sleep and effort. I think that after a semester of uncertainty about teaching, she is pleased with herself. My classes wrote generally satisfactory papers and ended the semester with a very lively debate concerning their group projects. I was not entirely satisfied with my ability to teach them, but virtually every one of them thanked me individually for turning them on intellectually. They were, I think, shaken a bit by what they could grasp of Freud and Nietzsche.

Karen's encounter group is completed as scheduled. She apparently gained two or three friends and admirers and perhaps a rather attractive female lover, who was the group leader. The girl is a pleasant sort who is pursuing Karen rather actively. This Karen finds satisfying, although they have not yet consummated their relationship sexualy. The girl's husband is probably bisexual also but is rather uptight about having his wife spend any time over here. He approves or at least tolerates (is probably intrigued by) the relationship between the girls but, I suspect, doesn't want her to have anything to do with me. A pity. I like her. She is a junior college teacher, and I find her interesting.

We are having an open house tomorrow with friends from a variety of circles coming. It should make for an interesting little social arena. I suspect some of our friends will scare some of the others. Amy and Karen planned the whole thing, which pleases me a great deal. It is gratifying to see them reach out. I think of our home as a little haven of freedom where opinions of any sort may be freely expressed and the only behavior condemned is that which is inhibited or causes pain to others. It will likely turn into a party in the evening, and I always enjoy having my friends over and seeing them relax and shake off a few of the cares and inhibitions with which they generally live.

I cannot refrain from remarking upon a contrast which was made evident today by the receipt of a Christmas gift from my parents. They sent a check for fifty dollars to the *three of us,* which showed their acceptance, not to say approval, of us as a group. This is to be contrasted with the secretive and virtually deceitful manner we have been forced to adopt with Amy's parents. And of course Karen's family knows nothing of the arrangement. It is really sad, for while it does not keep us from being together, it forces us to be apart from others, friends and family, whose feelings we value. We knew from the beginning that our experiment would set us apart from others. I am by no means bitter about it, since they are not my family and it is my parents who, while not wholly comprehending our behavior, give us some support from afar. What ill feelings I do have are directed toward an amorphous thing called Western Christian culture, toward the hypocrisy, the lack of understanding, the unwillingness to deviate, toward the repressive elements which make this society what it is.

Many of my thoughts this afternoon are of persons I love, not only Amy and Karen but also Joyce and Kim and Kathy. How I wish they could all be here for a while! Lovely creatures every one, each a part of me, my history, my personality, my world. I have said many times that women are my reality principle. Only Amy and Kim understand my meaning when I say it. They are energy, life, beauty.

AMY

Saturday, December 26 The fall semester at Stanford ended last week with a pile of exams it took me two days and all of one night to grade and turn in before leaving for four days in southern California with Rich and my mother. It was our Christmas gift from Mother, a total vacation, complete with fresh air, exercise, and good food. We rode horseback morning and afternoon and loved it, riding rain and shine. It was the first time that Rich and Karen and I have been separated since we came together on July 4, more than six months ago. The relationship between Rich and I is still much closer than that between Rich and Karen or Karen and me, and the permanency of our threesome is still uncertain.

Karen was lonely in the house while we were gone, in the sense that you're used to there being someone home when you get home, but she was busy during our absence spending time with Andy and Fred and old girl friends. Not having as close a relationship with Karen as we had hoped for, not sharing our most joyful times and most intimate secrets with each other, I think Rich and I have resented Karen's other relationships all along.

We returned on Tuesday and celebrated Christmas Eve together on Thursday. It was strange, buoyed up by effort and characterized by expected sentiments which didn't quite ring true. We had planned to spend the early evening with Sara, Sam, and Jamie at their house, celebrating the occasion with the only other marriage of our kind we've known for any length of time, and then return home to open our presents together. The evening was tranquil and pleasant, with fire and tree trimming and making of popcorn strands. Sam, with his Spanish upbringing and his personal sensitivity, is always so thoroughly warm and hospitable. He poured Karen and me eggnogs in a pair of gold metal goblets, and we relaxed into the tranquillity of their home.

Before we had left for their place, a funny thing happened.

Rich, lover that he is, surprised us with boxes of long-stemmed roses, yellow for me and red for Karen, as they had been last summer when we arrived. They were not really appreciated. We put them in vases, not arranging each one in delight as before, but sticking them in water to arrange later. But we never did.

Things were not right between us, but none of us had yet disclosed to the others or perhaps even admitted to ourselves that something was wrong. When things should have been fun, they weren't. When work should have gotten done, it didn't. When sex should develop, it didn't. On and on it went.

Later, back at our house, we opened our presents. Rich tried to put his finger on what was troubling us. He started asking us, "What's the matter with you two? What are you doing? Something's funny here." And Karen and I fended him off, attempting to deny and attempting to ward off the blow to our artificial bubble for the holiday occasion. You can't open presents in gloom and anger, so we had been consciously trying to create the mood that goes with presents without really feeling it. Rich took the wind out of our puffed-up sails, and did we each feel deflated! We weren't in cahoots; we just were each doing the same thing. It was questionable whether the evening would be redeemed and whether we would be able to continue opening our presents to each other, but I made the effort to reintroduce the determined lightheartedness, and each of them soon joined in with me, probably knowing that to do anything else was hopeless. The oohs and ahs and thanks for the presents all seemed phony and like empty, unfelt roles. Sometimes present opening is a little letdown just because of the big buildup to the occasion, but this time, it was more like a thud. We hadn't enjoyed our first Christmas, and if you don't enjoy the *first,* what the hell have you got to look forward to? The whole thing hadn't come off, and each of us felt the significance of that, though we did not talk about it together. So great the gap.

Christmas Day we had planned an open house. "From four to seven, as Karen has specified when inviting people, to which Rich has responded with "Why till seven? Why set a time for them to leave?" The open house was our way out of a Christmas dinner fiasco like we'd had at Thanksgiving. We just didn't have close friends in common to invite, so we invited a whole variety of people. At the open house, until late in the evening, Karen felt stiff and uncomfortable. Yet, she knew the people as well as I did. We had not drawn from the people we usually saw at parties that Karen didn't like; we had invited other people who teach with me at school, people we hadn't seen for a while, and friends that Karen wanted. She is almost always socially uptight and out of place. Later in the evening, after most of the people had left, there were eleven of us remaining who know each other reasonably well and who were all feeling close. Karen had opened up for a long time to Sid earlier in the evening, a real breakthrough for her with our friends, and then she and Sam talked intimately and honestly in the living room later. She was quite taken with Sam's insight and warmth and understanding, and so were several of the others here. Sid and Chris and Kay and Randy, a foursome, showed interest in Sara and Sam and Jamie, a threesome, as a result of listening to Sam talk and getting to know them this evening. Great interest was spontaneously generated in our putting together an encounter group made up of the three different groups of us to deal with the trials and tribulations of group living. It was a very satisfying, emotionally intense evening, worth much more than most social evenings have been for some time.

So now it is the day after Christmas. To my surprise, Karen came in at 11:00 A.M. and woke me up by making love to me! Good feelings and hope had developed last night. The encounter group proposal gave us something to look forward to, a way of trying to learn to get along with each other better. The evening had been an emotional high. What a pleasant awakening it was! We both thoroughly enjoyed it, and it was the most active and passionate that she and I have ever been with each other. After that, we both glowed most of the day. Rich and Karen were feeling alienated and had been for several days; she expressed her feelings by bitching to him about putting the toilet seat down and not leaving a trail of his clothes behind him, and he had sought peace by withdrawing from her. Karen, it seemed, was turning to me as she turned away from him. We had planned on the three of us going to see *Catch-22* this evening, but Rich wanted to think and write; mostly I think he just felt like he didn't want to be with Karen. So she and I went together, feeling very much the other's date after the morning's lovemaking. We held hands in the movie and touched one another's legs and felt the inhibition imposed on two girls holding hands, whereas no thought is given to girls and guys holding hands. No one said or did anything to us, but we both were conscious that some of the people sitting around us had probably noticed. It was a feeling to experience and explore, rather than retreat from, so we held hands through the whole show.

KAREN

Monday, December 28 I'm sick; sick at my stomach, sick of my head, sick of me. I feel very strange: shaky and yet calm at the same time. I'm feeling extremely hostile, estranged, and alienated from Rich. I don't know when it started; he's been different since the acid trip. I'm reacting very strongly to very petty things, so there must be a deeper reason, but I don't know what or why. On January 4, I will have been with Rich and Amy for six months. That's a short time to change so much. Oh, I have good intentions, all right, but a hell of a lot of good they do me! I'm still hung up; I'm still insecure; I'm still jealous. Sometimes I wonder if it's worth all the fright I'm going through—being shattered like this. It hurts so much sometimes I think of jerking the steering wheel and tumbling over an embankment or into a stone wall just to have a scale on which to register hurts. How can anyone possibly know about the pain inside? How can *I* know what someone else is feeling? It's hypocritical to say,

"I understand." I don't. If I did, I'd be coping better. I now doubt that I'll ever be able to not care if Amy makes love to Joyce or Rich fucks every girl in Palo Alto. And I'm not capable of facing the rest of my life with the gut-twisting feelings I have inside now.

It seems like we go from one crisis into another. If it isn't Rich, it's Amy; and if it isn't Amy, it's me; and I'm more often the cause than anything else. Rich and Amy appear to have bitten off more than they can chew, literally. Did I deceive them; did I lead them to believe I was further along than I really am? Now they're impatient and straining at the bit to go ahead. I feel left to make it on my own, with occasional pats on the head. That's the way it always is. Alone. And I keep getting taken in and believing you really can share. Bullshit! You make it on your own, baby, or not at all 'cause no one else really gives a damn, not really deep down inside. It's against human nature. Everyone looks out for himself, and perhaps that's the way, the only way. Hell, if you can't help yourself, how can you ever help anyone else? Besides, how can anyone else possibly know your pace and when you pass certain points; who wants to backtrack for someone else? NOBODY!

What am I doing here
Why do I keep fucking up their world
It's blowing my mind
What mind
Maybe I was born without one
Finger, toe missing
Why not mind missing

Hurt hurts more than pleasure pleases
If pleasure soothes hurt does hurt wipe out pleasure
Could I stick up for my beliefs, convictions,
        feelings, conclusions myself if I found them

Where will I be when I find my head
Esteem self low high self esteem
Dancing in twilight zone out of reach
Why?

RICH

Wednesday, December 30 Tennessee Williams says he is particularly interested in the communal efforts of young people in breaking up the old-style uptight family structure.

> "Oh, I don't think I could live in a commune myself or even in what they call a 'triangular marriage'—you know, one guy with two chicks. I'm too jealous by nature. . . .
>
> "But it's so marvelously exciting. Everything is changing so rapidly. We're on the verge, I think, of a social revolution."
>
> He laughed again. "I can't wait, you know, to get back to my TV set to see what happens next," he said. (*San Francisco Chronicle,* 12/30/70)

Williams is on the right track, though he is employing or observing the wrong medium. While it is no doubt true that there will one day be a drama or situation comedy series based on a threesome, he is surely aware that the "verge" he speaks of is being actualized already. Other writers (among them Margaret Mead, Richard Farson, Sam Keen, Albert Ellis) are also becoming aware of such changes and coming practices. They all try hard to stay in touch, as good scientists and authors should; but I fear more what they fail to see, fail to appreciate, fail to comprehend. They are, every one, conservative in their opinions and expectations. And no one yet has studied group marriage in this society, save for a lone young couple in the East, Larry and Joan Constantine.

AMY

Saturday, January 2 We had a full New Year's Eve, and I'm not sure where things stand with Karen and us just now, except to say that I feel distance both from and toward her. We went to a small New Year's Eve party at Sid and Chris and Kay and Randy's; there were only nine of us (the three of us and Abe and Maggie). We spent the night, all tripping together (this time just for fun) and in our own little groups. Karen had a cold, so she only took a little pinch of acid. I was enjoying my environment and just having a nice time until Rich and Karen came to get me to join their talk.

Karen was crying and feeling sorry for herself and nostalgic for Brian, her old boyfriend, who I found out then had earlier asked her out for New Year's Eve. That was the first I had heard of that! From the conversation that ensued, it seemed apparent to me that Karen was really unsure about her feelings for us and was seriously considering beating a retreat to Brian. I felt betrayed. Not that she might go to Brian, but that she really had been hiding her feelings from us, and that wasn't fair to us. God help me, I'm coming to have occasional feelings of being taken, though not intentionally. We used to argue jokingly over which one of us had the best deal; well, now it's becoming more of a question of which one's getting the *worst* deal or the short end of the stick. I think each one of us feels that way now.

We finally slept, and Friday each of us arose when we felt like it and joined the crowd in front of the color TV watching bowl games, one after the other after the other. Karen seemed almost pathetically out of place to me, and I felt certain she felt lonely and like she didn't really belong there. I wanted to comfort her, but I felt a sense of finality.

RICH

Saturday, January 2 Our future as a group seems less and less certain. A number of things have happened, and several feelings have emerged that threaten us. It is difficult to be objective, and perhaps I ought not to try to be. What is odd is that the problems which plague us are, not specifically problems which arise from what I take to be the nature and structure of the three-person group, but are rather the sort of thing which any two persons might encounter. Overall, I see it as the result of a strain imposed by differential growth. In a word, Karen always acts under pressure because she is always attempting to catch up with Amy and me. Her style and pace and manner do not fit at all comfortably with those which Amy and I have developed. This is no peculiar fault of hers, only perhaps that she overestimated her capacity to adapt. Nor is it that I—or Amy—are to blame. Perhaps only that I did not try hard enough or love freely enough or that my social magic was not enough to draw Karen out, to chase away the feelings of inadequacies, to boost the low self-esteem.

I am not a very good companion to her. Not at that everyday, you-me level where one seeks out the company of the other for the mere pleasure of being with them. Not at the level where trivial facts assume great weight because they are a part of the biography of someone you love. Not at the level where the little hurts are always worth soothing. Not at the level of ice-cream cones, postcards, and shared phone calls with friends.

Nor is she a real, true companion to me. If ever she might have been (when we met in Los Angeles), I missed it because I did not spend a great deal of time with her, and I have changed a good deal since then.

She also still harbors a hurt and rejected love for Brian. She has deep feelings of love and respect for Amy and me, but Brian captured her heart long ago. The wounds of his indifference have not healed. She misses him but now feels repelled by his straight existence, his devotion to his career (which he puts first), and his need for a perfect wife who is always there *when he needs her* but who finds him preoccupied when she needs him. If she feels that much for him, I truly think she belongs with him, though I doubt they will be happy unless and until he grows up and opens up. I love her sufficiently to want her to be happy. I shall miss her if we do break up, though it is true I have felt inhibited by her presence from time to time. I have also felt much pleasure at seeing her grow, for she surely has—to the point of seeing the nine to five, fifty weeks a year, split level in the suburbs till age sixty-five as a great compromise, a truly limited existence. She has been challenged on many fronts—emotionally, socially, sexually, intellectually—and, though threatened, has come to a better understanding of herself. But at this point in her life, the challenges may be overwhelming her, and my love may not be enough to help her meet them. A group marriage may not fit into her personality structure; and even if it did, Amy and I may not be the right ones for sustaining such a relationship.

I think we would all benefit—and perhaps others as well, for there will surely be others to try it in as many ways as there are family and group and personality structures—if we would each search ourselves for the reasons for our apparent failure. I say *apparent,* since I am convinced that we have each benefited from the experience. I know Karen better. I know Amy better. I certainly know myself better. That is reason enough for such a venture. And perhaps, just perhaps, we might find some solution that would help us stay together or at least aid us in making a responsible, unselfish, rational decision to discontinue. The mysteries of group love and of companionship are worth exploring in any case.

Six months seems such a short time, and yet we have learned and shared so much! Perhaps I am only seeking rationalizations, but no genuine experiment of this nature could ever be a failure. Every person must be moved by the experience, if not to total self-comprehension at least to an expansion of self-awareness. His history has been altered; his personal development, challenged. The monogamic, dyadic, nuclear family will never look quite the same to me. Communes, kibbutzim, and tribes will have a different meaning as a possible alternative for daily life. Hippie cults I will regard not, as groups of freaks, but as possible bands of social rebels seeking a better way, albeit often in the dark. Multiple love I will regard, not as a far-out idea, or even as a way of relating to a group of disparate persons, but as a possible orienting force for daily existence. Nor will love for another man be a threat. I now regard bisexuality as the achievement of a truly integrated sexuality. These things I learned from Amy and Karen, although neither of them is aware of the precise and complete effect of their lives on me.

And I have learned more than I ever knew about jealousy and personal insecurity, about privacy and flexibility, about interpersonal communication, and about feminine nature and interaction, and many more things.

Tuesday, January 12 Our little group appears to be headed for a sad end. The conflicts and disappointments, especially between Karen and me, seem too great and too depressing to continue. We have all tried to resolve issues, improve communication, and become more intimate, but for a number of reasons—reasons which should be spelled out here as thoroughly as I can manage—it seems best that we part, which means that Karen will be moving out as soon as it is feasible for her. She has begun her new job, and while it is an added pressure during a depressing period of disillusionment, it will likely make her feel more capable and independent. She will actually be working with the same boss and almost the same staff as in Dallas. She is now taking the job we talked her out of in the fall.

Despite the conflicts and the alienation to which it has led currently, I still feel love for Karen. I still feel a certain obligation for her welfare and happiness. But it is not merely an obligation that I feel, I also feel a desire for her, a desire for her physically and a desire to see her mature and develop into the best person she is capable of becoming. I press on people very hard for that development. It is the reason for some of the conflicts which exist between Amy and me. Most of all, I feel I push myself. I am to some extent hypocritical. But it has always seemed a waste to me of the greatest moment and of the greatest significance to squander one's personal attributes. I believe I am not being merely self-righteous when I push on other persons. As a matter of fact, I often do it, not merely for the sake of the other person, but in order to have bigger and better playmates for myself.

Karen has fluctuated in her response to these needs which exist in me. I do not condemn her for that inconstancy, for it is indeed one I find myself slipping into, but only occasionally. I feel as though I am, as Wilhelm Reich's wife said of him, "outside the trap." Being "outside the trap" is a source of conflict in a backhanded sort of way between myself and other persons. I am sure that I strike them as overbearing, constantly demanding, and sometimes downright pompous. In truth, I am seeking merely to find companions to share the intellectual world with me without an academic structure. In truth, I feel less and less like I need an institutional framework in which to do my own thinking. It would not be a convenient niche even if I could find one. Frameworks constrain, rules bind, especially when they are poorly conceived.

Throughout the last six months, the relationship between Amy and me has actually done nothing but improve, with occasional perturbations here and there. The alienation from Karen has only served to move me closer to Amy, who is most accepting of me in that way. I honestly believe that she feels no jealousy toward Karen and no hostility, only a measure of disappointment. Such a response is only a further indication of her stability and security, which is developing day by day, much to my joyous satisfaction. Next month she presents her first professional paper. I am proud to see her taking on such a challenge, and I will assist her in every way I can to help her carry it off successfully. Amy and I have a wonderful future ahead of us. It seems a pity that Karen cannot be a very intimate and full part of it, to share in what I feel is our great bounty.

That bounty will likely not be material nor physical in nature. It consists of a wonderful sense of satisfaction derived from a kind of interpersonal compatibility that she and I discovered some time ago. When we met in Los Angeles, it was to our great advantage that we were both somewhat committed in feeling to persons we had left at home. This commitment enabled us to be totally candid with each other in regard to our feelings due to the fact that we would be returning to our respective homes within a matter of months. That is to say, there was more reason to level with one another and nothing to be gained by wearing any masks as far as the other person was concerned.

Amy and I were fortunate in that we had in effect a trial marriage while we were in Los Angeles. In fact, when we came to the Bay Area, we married primarily for the convenience of it. We had traveled together, worked together, played together, loved together, and deeply entwined our personalities, indeed our souls, in the existence of the other person. How we should expect anyone to catch up with this phenomenon is a difficult question to face. I think that Karen tried her best.

I truly believe, and I set myself to the task, that the unexamined life is not worth living. Due to my socialization, my personality structure, and various characteristics in my lifestyle, most of my explorations and inquiries are into the psychic and social self. The past six months have indeed been a time for examination. Sometimes they were painful examinations; sometimes they were pointless examinations; other times they produced very useful results. I am more aware of some of my limitations, for example, that my personality, such as it was, was unable to reach out and unlock some of the fears and insecurities that lie deep within Karen. I am sad for this, too.

It would be fair to say that Karen simply got in over her head, that she didn't realize what she was getting into, and that she was not aware of what such an arrangement might lead to. If it has been painful for her, I suppose I am really glad that it is over.

Friday, January 15 Group marriages have been a common feature in many cultures of the past. There is no reason to think, other than for the cultural and social restrictions placed upon them by our current society, that they are not a viable social arrangement in the contemporary world or that they may not proliferate, probably in the not too distant future. I would say that within a generation they will begin to be accepted by the society at large—generally tolerated, if not approved—and will become institutionalized during the next century. That is to say, the requisite legal, social, political, and economic underpinnings of various forms of marriage will then be present. This will include everything from various kinds of welfare and life insurance plans to multiple corporate family holdings, which now exist over and above the nuclear and linear family system in twentieth-century America.

It is an eminently sensible way to live. For me, the greatest advantage is what I might call the *emotional pluralism*. I have known for some time that genuine multiple love is possible, that jealousy could in fact be overcome, and that jealousy itself was a learned and not an instinctual response. I would hypothesize that this is true both for animals and for human beings, despite the claims of the zoologists and comparative biologists in this area. And in any case, if it were instinctual, it would be necessary, given the development of the population and ecology problems alongside problems of territoriality and consumer neurosis, to resocialize the human species in order to allow them to live peaceably together.

The development of successful triadic love and family relationships might constitute a social breakthrough that will allow us to see a variety of such situations in a variety of kinds and sizes as reasonable and normal responses to a very complex social and technical world. It has usually been the case among utopian thinkers (I refer specifically to such men as Edward Bellamy, B. F. Skinner, and even the gloomy picture painted by Aldous Huxley in *Brave New World*) that they viewed social and cultural revolutions as taking place in the economic and technological sphere, meaning the outside framework of social action. Very few have thought of reforming the personality or the psychic structure first, attempting to reeducate it, bring it to an awareness of new possibilities, and lift its goals and aspirations for social life, thereby lifting the quality along with it and causing further changes in that institutional framework from which most thinkers begin. This is only a way of saying—to address myself to the contemporary world—that the revolution begins at home, in your own heart and mind.

The group marriage was my attempt to do so. In external terms, it has failed; and as one of my friends pointed out, we now join that great attrition among group marriages (of which there are very few to begin with) that makes the entire attempt look bad, even foolish. But the results cannot be a total failure, for there are no other results to compare with them. If I seem naïve, idealistic, or overly sanguine about the whole matter, it is because I now stand in a position of minimal experience. I have experienced the warm support and endearment of two wonderful women. I have known their caresses, their sexual excitement, and some of their personal faults. I have experienced the envy of other men, which I did not find entirely comfortable but in which, nonetheless, I took some pleasure. I have a new appreciation for sex, both my own and what is mistakenly called the *opposite.*

We know of two other group marriages which are currently working. It would be easy to say about both that they came together because of their insecurities. But such a view fails to probe beneath the surface, the surface of the second-rate clinical psychologists, the naïve assistance of the marriage counselors, who are usually called in only when the situation is desperate. It would be easy to say that all of these persons are kidding themselves, that all of them have some pathological preoccupation which draws them together, that they are obsessed with their own fears and insecurities, that they are sex perverts, etcetera. But such easy statements do not help us one whit in explaining why the possibility of group marriage would seem attractive to some as well as disgusting and repellent to others.

If I may be blunt and egotistical at the same time, I might say that my opinion is that persons who are willing to experiment with group living situations which include a significant level of sharing and intimacy, physical and otherwise—such persons are as important in their explorations and their experiments as any man who walks the surface of the moon or explores the depths of the sea. They are pioneers and revolutionaries at the same time, though often they are unaware of the historical role they are playing.

It is conceivable to me that the triad and the small group might be more stable, given the appropriate environment, than the dyad as we know it today. Heterosexual biology makes the dyad seem entirely normal and appropriate, but we should go beyond that basic biological type of thinking to explore the nature of our social institutions, which often include a third person—a judge, an arbitrator, a psychologist, an administrative assistant, etcetera—who mediates between the purposes and intents of other two-person groups. In this sense, the very essence of fairness is to have a third person present, especially to mediate a conflicting point of view and to open communication between two otherwise intransigent persons. We do not think of marriage in these terms, but George Bach's material included in *The Intimate Enemy* must make us aware of the subtle forms of conflict that are implicit in any two-person arrangements. It is his opinion that until we learn to resolve conflict between two persons and within small groups, we shall not understand how to deal with violence and conflict on the national and international scales that must be dealt with in the future. We always deem it fair and right and just to have an umpire of whatever sort wherever there is a contest taking place because where there is a contest for limited ends and goods, there is conflict between those who cannot both possess it. Whether this be an inevitable factor in marriage is something to be explored.

AMY

Tuesday, January 19 Thursday night I taught my last class for the fall semester at San Jose State. Karen wasn't there. The night before, she had gotten a pain in her chest and developed difficulty with her breathing. It bothered her all night, and in the morning I took her to the emergency room at the nearest hospital. The doctor, a really groovy young guy in brown wide-wale cords and a soft purple shirt, decided she might have a touch of pleurisy and gave her a pain-killer, but he said he had the feeling that the fact that she was supposed to start a new job the next day had something to do with it.

So Karen didn't make it to my class that night, and she didn't make it to the new job the next day, but she did make it out with Brian that night.

The next night, Saturday, Rich and I were going to attend a party that Karen didn't care to go to, and we had arranged to have Joyce come over and join us for dinner and the evening. Karen's been jealous of Joyce all along, and we had all but given Joyce up for Karen. Somehow that hadn't seemed right or justified anymore. About 9:30, Karen came out of her room with a slight stomping flavor and asked how soon we were leaving for the party. I said as soon as I could get my hair done. I had the feeling she was getting impatient to get us out of the house. Well, sure enough! When we left, about ten minutes later, I went in to say good-bye to her and to ask her if she was mad about something or if something was bothering her. At first she said no, in her typical communication-inhibitor move; but when pressed, she exploded that if Joyce wasn't out of here in five minutes, she was going to throw her out! I felt astonishment and anger. She looked so uptight, there was nothing to be said; there was no chance of communicating. We left, and I told Rich and Joyce in the car why I was upset and shattered-looking.

What had hit me in the face was the intensity and frequency of her defensiveness. It's tiring; I mean, it physically wears one out to try to cope with it, and I'm sure the defenses sap a lot of her energy. The task is too big for us. Can't she ever let us have a relaxed evening, with or without her, without having to worry about her being uptight about something? I really resented what she had said.

When we arrived at the party, I felt comfortable and really relaxed from the moment we walked in the door, and I felt that way all evening. Rich and I and Joyce went back over with Maggie to her place at three in the morning to have some breakfast. Rich didn't want to go home, and we were awfully tired, so we all just went to sleep there and came home the next morning at 11:00.

We had had a falling out earlier in the week, almost calling a halt to the threesome, but had agreed to think about what our feelings were and what we wanted for a few days. Karen didn't know whether she wanted to continue with us, and we didn't know that we wanted her to. We had all discussed how Rich wasn't satisfying her romantic needs and how she didn't think she was making any progress with her insecurities and defenses. She was very discouraged. That Saturday evening, Rich and I had seen and felt the contrast between a relaxed evening and the kind we spent when Karen was with us. I think that turned the trick. By the time we came home that morning, we knew it was over.

When we got home, Karen was sullen and distant. After a brief exchange, Rich and I went to bed to get some more sleep. I fell asleep, but he couldn't, so he went to have it out with her. When I woke up, it had been decided that she was going to move out. I felt strangely displaced and up in the air about where things stood with her, how she felt about it all, and what I should say to her. It was strange not to be there when the end came. I'm sure Rich thought he was making it easier for me by my not being there at a time which was bound to be a sad one. My not being there at that time may be part of why she is not so alienated from me now, not hostile toward me in the same way that she is toward Rich.

Monday, January 25 Since we made the break, we have seen very little of Karen, though she has not yet moved out. She has not felt like she belongs here anymore. She has felt so much hurt and failure and inadequacy that she has withdrawn almost completely from us and has chosen to escape from the environment here, mostly seeking solace with the familiarity of Brian, despite her previous frustration and dissatisfaction with her life with him, from which she had fled only six months ago to our arms and our home. She has found an apartment of her own in Menlo Park and will begin to move her things out on February 1.

RICH

Thursday, January 28 A sense of finality pervades my mood, which is depressed and sad and yet relieved that the pressures of our experiment will soon disappear. There are many, many thoughts in my mind, each crowding the other, calling for attention and expression. I am tempted to be melodramatic and effusive with regard to my own feelings. I guess I would prefer the more rewarding reflections involved in a post hoc diagnosis of our group. I am not one for self-pity.

Kurt Lewin remarks somewhere that every person has his own need for social space, which will differ from that of every other person according to his activity level. For example, Karen and Amy had their need for solitude and therapeutic withdrawal. They require a domestic organization that allows them to have their privacy when they opt for it. With respect to me, I have a very high and very active sex drive, and therefore two female sexual partners seem ideal to me. I have, as the Freudians would say, a large and active libido. This libido, however, is not restricted to sexual activity alone, as any good psychoanalyst knows. It includes my entire life space, and I try to function within it. I would say that I have a large need for ideological space, rather than a need to acquire territory itself. The latter quality is found in the actions of many, if not most, men.

I take little satisfaction in the fact that we as a group outlasted a certain percentage of the dyadic, heterosexual, monogamic marital arrangements that are the sum and substance of our culture. It is well known that most marriages which are destined to dissolve do so in the first year. This, of course, is what has happened to us. It was a trial marriage; it was an experiment, but a very serious and personal one as well. I pray that it leaves scars on no one, though I have some fear for that where Karen is concerned. If on occasion I sound somewhat dry and analytic in my comments, perhaps that is only my own defense mechanism coming to the fore, allowing me to rationalize in a very special way the entire experience. Being academically oriented, I suppose this is my prerogative; for indeed, it is one way of coping with the world.

Marriage itself is a way of coping with the world if seen from the proper perspective. The pressures on the dyadic marital arrangement put it in such tremendous danger that we have been witnessing, not its decline, but its disastrous breakdown over the last two generations. If we do not move toward *altered* marital and familial arrangements *now*—not in the very near future, as some would urge upon us—we shall be visited with a large number of dire consequences, including suicide, mental illness, desertion, and so forth, at a rate that we never knew was possible before. Does this mean that the divorce rate will continue to rise? Yes, I think so, but that is merely one indicator and possibly not even the best one, even though it is the most easily recorded.

No one knows how much misery and personal damage is caused by the inability of individuals to satisfactorily adjust to the dyadic family arrangement. It is a highly restrictive mold, one which circumscribes one's emotional potential especially. The roles it prescribes for the male and the female are themselves very rigid and limited and tend to generate expectations that few mortals are really capable of attaining. My experiences with Amy and Karen have allowed me to see new and very practical possibilities along these lines. If only I could see them practiced elsewhere, then I might get a better understanding of those possibilities in relation to concrete personality structures and the social environment we find ourselves in in the modern world. This is no utopian dream, but a practical necessity if we are not to be faced with the consequences of the breakdown of one of our basic institutions.

Saturday, February 13 As I have searched my memory to determine the precise point at which my attitudes toward Karen might have changed, I have found two significant incidents which help account for our present difficulties and soon-to-be-terminated arrangement.

The first was, not an incident, but the lack of a series of incidents. Karen had planned at the beginning of the semester to take some time and visit the Stanford campus to explore what I think are some of the finest classes and some of the finest lectures to be found anywhere in the world. I told her that she had one of the best universities in the country a few blocks away and that merely by dropping in there, she could gain a great deal of knowledge and help to find herself, intellectually, at least. This she never did. This disappointed me.

Secondly, she once made a comment, sometime in November, I believe, to the effect that she felt as though she were a "kept woman." The comment stunned me somewhat. It was another manifestation of her low self-esteem, her feeling of not being worthy and able to fit in and catch up. I told her a long time ago, through tapes and letters, that I was not just looking to "keep a woman on the side." I was not so much interested in having two sexual partners as I was in having two mature and affectionate companions whom I could respect and rely on. That comment of hers let me know that she felt a certain relationship of dependence that I found uncomfortable and, indeed, objected to. It is possible that this has colored my responses ever since.

What convinces me of the rightness of our breakup at this point is the fact that Karen has so totally withdrawn. She is, indeed, completely alienated insofar as I am concerned, and I believe she is moving farther away from Amy to fortify her own defenses, not realizing that both Amy and I want to help as much as we can. The fact that she cannot cope with the negative feelings that she is having, that she cannot communicate them to us satisfactorily, and that she cannot come to terms with us even while we are parting is indicative in retrospect of the fact that she could not have related to me very well in the long run. I often think how much pain and loneliness she must be feeling now, for she is spending nearly every night out—with a friend, of course, but from what she has told me previously, not with friends she feels terribly deeply for. She is, in a word, using them to support her in a time of crisis. I approve of this. I am glad they are there for her. I only wish she would try to draw a little sustenance from me, as I still feel willing to give it.

Amy and I are getting along wonderfully well, even though the pressure of our own lives has increased proportionate to Karen's exit from our life space. Next week Amy and I fly to Boston to give a professional paper. It should be an exciting time for us. We have been working on the paper and are really looking forward to giving it. Amy's confidence has been boosted by the whole experience. When we return, Karen will be gone, and we shall likely start a new phase of our life together. That's the way it goes: constant renewal, constant exploration, inconstant growth, and a great deal of life to live. There is so much to know and so much to do that one hardly knows where to begin. And in the beginning, one rarely knows just when the beginning begins.

Karen could have been so much a part of it had she wished. She has a great deal to offer, but in many ways she hardly knows how to extend and develop herself according to her own needs and her own values. She has never seen clearly or for an extended length of time my need for her. Perhaps somewhere deep down inside, she rejects that need because she realizes that she would always have to share it with Amy. Perhaps she was always meant for one man but has not yet found him, though I think this in general runs counter to the foundations of human nature.

Thursday, February 25 For a brief, oh so brief, span of time, I had them both.

Amy and I arrived from Boston last Monday evening. Karen picked us up at the airport and dropped us off at another friend's house so that we could get our car. When we returned to the house, all of her belongings were gone. The house just seemed a little less filled with life.

In the few days since then, Amy has seemed noticeably busier, since many tasks that she and Karen once shared are now back squarely upon her shoulders. I am trying to help her as much as I can, but I am sometimes clumsy about it. At the same time, there is a different sense of privacy about the house. It is not simply that it is less crowded—that's not quite the point—but rather that privacy is more accessible and one's life space is less intruded upon in unanticipated ways.

Karen was congenial enough when she picked us up at the

airport, but I had the distinct feeling of a deep hurt and resentment lying somewhere in her. At the same time, she is now faced with a new set of challenges and responsibilities. She is also involved with three men, and I wonder sometimes if she is not merely bouncing about.

My speculations and reflections concerning our demise as a group marriage lead me now to see it as the result of a lack of sufficient multiple interdependency, which must be the basis of any marriage and therefore the basis of any group marriage. There must be needs which extend from each person to each other person in the group, needs which are then appropriately responded to insofar as the other party is able.

KAREN

Tuesday, March 16 It's like I'm back at the beginning again, starting all over again. Except it's not the same; nothing is the same. Rich, Amy, and I are no longer a family. I'm not sure what we are.

I couldn't write about it till now. And even yet, I have a crummy feeling in the pit of my stomach and in the center of my heart.

My observations and examinations will be different, of course, now than if I had written them at the time. That can't be helped. The pain was too much; it shook my very core, and just now, two months after leaving, has it become dulled.

Just before Christmas, we got a letter from Kim. She was so depressed and lonely that we discussed having her down for Christmas. We all discussed the pros and cons. Amy was utterly swamped. She had work to catch up on, papers to grade, the trip to the ranch, and more.

Anyway, the tension was quite high. She was really upset,

and in the midst of it all, she told Rich she thought perhaps he preferred me. She didn't understand his extreme reactions (yelling, fighting more, etcetera) since I'd been there. She said sometimes she even felt like taking the total cop-out, meaning suicide. Rich called me into the room and made her repeat it. I was totally flabbergasted. Rich prefer me—jeez! I simply couldn't comprehend her having those feelings, perhaps just as she couldn't understand some of mine. And as for suicide—Well, Amy later told me she really didn't mean that. That perhaps it was a culmination of total frustration at all the things happening to her and the fact that we weren't all getting it together and maybe just a little bit for shock value. She doesn't resort to such ploys as much as most people; actually, that's the first time I'd heard her say anything that would fall into that category.

Christmas was really bad news. Lots of pressures put a strain on all of us. Rich sent us roses again. They were as gorgeous as the first ones had been, but something wasn't the same, though I can't say what that something was. Could it have been the end, the alpha and omega, the beginning and the end? I'm sure that's not what he had in mind.

Tension between Rich and me continued to grow—sometimes more and sometimes less, but always there. I felt closer to Amy for a while. I thought it was mutual at the time, but as I reflect on it now, I can't help but think part of it was that she was simply and perhaps unconsciously (perhaps consciously) providing a buffer zone. Strange how at the beginning we related through Rich and at the end I related directly to Amy, excluding Rich. Well, not really excluding him; it's just that I didn't feel close.

I had a jim-dandy cold (flu) over New Year's. We went to Sid and Chris and Kay and Randy's and were joined there by Abe and Maggie. I felt absolutely rotten (per usual when I have a cold) but enjoyed myself. We watched TV and ate, and watched TV and ate. Rich and Amy tripped, and Rich

and I began talking about why we all three weren't close.
Things got pretty heavy. We caught Amy as she walked
through the room and asked her to go upstairs to talk. She
acted strange, and Rich talked to her, stressing the importance of what we were discussing. We all went upstairs and
talked. I was straight because of my run-down physical con-
dition due to the cold. But our discussion was somewhat
strange. Sometimes I couldn't really tell what Amy was
thinking or feeling. Even her speech pattern (so many hesita-
tions, ahs and ums) tells me she screens *everything* and
doesn't come out or let go with all she's thinking and feeling,
even on acid, and I felt it *especially* New Year's Eve night.
I could only flashback to her expression that Rich preferred
me, and that seemed tinged with resentment. Not that he
preferred me—that's simply absurd—but that either she resented my moving in with them from the beginning (which
I don't think is the case) *or,* and probably more likely, she
was tired of the tension and constant hassles I was causing.

I don't know exactly when I began feeling this way, but
I know that by December, I was very aware of feeling extra,
like an addition. Sometimes I wonder if Amy really wanted
me all along. I have to again go back to her remarks about
Rich preferring me and we had so much in common (or
something to that effect). The whole six months viewed from
the perspective of that statement suggests that perhaps there
was indirect or unconscious pressure on her to go along with
the idea whether she wanted to or not. If she objected to
begin with, she would have Rich to contend with, and he can
be so unrelenting. And I don't see her as denying him anything so long as she has a few comforts along the way. I see
him as perhaps talking her into it directly or indirectly. She
always talks about not wanting to be "staid," but she fights
the hardest against change. That always struck me as funny.
If it weren't for Rich constantly pulling and dragging her
along, she would be "staid" in her own way. That seems, at
least to me, to be one of the beautiful things about their

relationship. She is just enough gravity on him to keep him
—what? Sane? It works for them.

On January 8, I was to start to work with the company I
worked for in Dallas, but this time at their San Francisco
office. On January 6, I had very funny pains in my chest. I
thought it was an apple or pear I had eaten too quickly on
the way home from class, but it didn't go away. I didn't sleep
that night, and by the morning of the seventh, I couldn't
stand it, and Amy took me to the hospital. I had a case of
pleurisy resulting from the bad cold I had the previous week
over the holidays. I missed classes that day and just stayed
in bed and rested. I felt better the next day and kind of
restless. On Saturday Amy had invited Joyce over for dinner
before she, Joyce, and Rich went to a party. I was still
working on a paper and thought I'd finish it up while they
were at the party. I still have a thing about Joyce. I just don't
like her; she offends me. She came for dinner, and things
were fine. As the evening wore on, the "things were fine"
wore thin. By the time dinner was over, I had had all of Joyce
I could take in one dose. I dislike her, and while I try, the
longer I'm around her, the more intense my feelings get.
That's what happened; actually I was a bit surprised at my
own reaction. Well, that ended the evening right there. Rich
and Amy and Joyce left shortly after my explosive demand
that Amy and Joyce get out of the house because I couldn't
stand it another minute. I assume she told them what happened and that explains why they didn't return that night.
I felt worse as it got later. I couldn't concentrate on my
paper. They finally came home about 11:00 A.M. Sunday.
Everything was strained. Rich and Amy tried to sleep, but
he couldn't sleep and came into my room to talk. We decided
we were all too miserable to continue. I said, "I think I'd
better leave," and he agreed.

So, six months and two days after its formation, the group
marriage dissolved.

Even as Rich and I were sitting in my room looking at each other, I knew what was happening and what the outcome would be, and I still couldn't believe it was real. I felt outwardly calm, but I knew it wouldn't last long as I left the house to get a newspaper. As soon as I walked out of the house, it hit me, and I started to feel all shaky and fragmented inside. I have never in my life felt so all alone. There were people I could have called, but somehow it wouldn't have helped. The feelings were so tied up inside of me and my life of the past six months that I would have been hard put to have expressed in words the thousands of things going through me.

I am still in the process of sorting those thousands of things out. It doesn't hurt with the intensity it did at first. Am I becoming hardened? Withdrawn? Or am I really coping and coming to grips with reality?

I have given the incident (the last straw, as it were) with Joyce a great deal of thought. My feelings have settled to a point where I can say I just don't care for her as a person, and I feel a tiny bit of resentment at the pressure applied on me to like her. Simply saying "give her a chance" was pressure, in a way. What I mean is that I never felt that I should or wanted to force my friends on them, and I was even willing to give them up. That was a contributing factor in my not seeing Andy as much as I would have liked. Andy didn't understand, and Rich didn't understand, and I felt caught in the middle. I just couldn't juggle two heavy emotional and sexual involvements at one time. So Andy just sort of floated in and out of the picture. He tried to understand, and yet now I realize how very difficult a thing it is to be told that someone is attached and involved and yet free to know and care for others and yet to find oneself always seemingly on the fringes of that person's life. What an uncomfortable position that must have been for him.

Back to the thing with Joyce. I also felt the pressure because I was constantly put in the presence (at parties, etcetera) of their friends of many years' standing. These friends naturally included Joyce. I truly felt at a loss as to how to make new friends, and as I now see it, I was satisfying myself through outside friendships with Andy, Fred, and others. I was absolutely blank when it came to thinking up ways to make friends for the three of us. At first I was dubious of the ad we placed in the local underground paper, but I came to see it as an effective way of presenting ourselves as a three-some and of finding some playmates. We got lots of re-sponses, but that kind of petered out too. Our relationship had started to deteriorate to a marked degree by that time and rapidly grew worse before we could take any real action on the responses.

I'm not sure, but I think possibly the biggest factor in my feeling threatened by Joyce is that she was Amy's first lover. I think that accounts for well over half of my hostile feelings toward her. The rest can be accounted for by saying she talks too much. She doesn't shut up for one minute from the time she walks in the door. Whatever you talk about, she knows something about it or someone who did it. I simply can't believe that someone can be *that* interested and *that* tuned in. I'm always ready to listen to what someone has to say, and it irritates me when someone else has all the answers. That's precisely the way Joyce strikes me. I can't ignore the possibility, though, that I'm jealous. She's attractive and has a nice figure, and she seems to be relatively uninhibited.

There were a few other incidences which really turned me off. For example, she once remarked to Rich: "If things don't work out with Karen, I'll be glad to move in." I don't know what there is left to say about her. I wish I had been a little thicker skinned when it came to her. I wish I had been able to accept her and her relationship with Rich and Amy and not let her get to me. Hang-ups—sure—but everybody has 'em.

I must reflect on the whole six months now and try to tie some of the loose threads together. I have to inquire now whether I'm (now, ever have been, or ever will be) mentally or emotionally suited for a threesome relationship. I realize now how very socialized I am for pairs, couples, and one-to-one relationships. I can visualize realistically the many disadvantages and limitations of a couple isolated in a house and having to function and interact with each other by today's standards and demands. But seemingly no amount of telling myself and pointing out the rational aspects of group marriages will dispel the feelings of insecurity I had. If I had the time and a good listener, I suppose I could dig up a few reasons via childhood experiences and family-marriage models, most of which were nonsharing, socially isolated, and unrealistic. I do, however, see group marriages becoming more common and workable but perhaps with certain factors different from what was true of our situation. The persons involved would be younger, perhaps more similar in family background, and most important, would all come together at one time rather than (especially in the case of threesomes) one added on.

After the end had come, I began looking for an apartment. I was also working part-time for my old boss Jason. He kept giving me all this stand-up-for-yourself kind of gritty advice, which was just the very last thing in the world I needed at the time. I felt exposed and bruised and battered and weary and just like crawling inside myself for a few months to heal. Instead, he kept giving me stick-your-chin-out-and-get-back-in-the-mainstream-of-life stuff that only served to make me withdraw more. He did, however, sit and talk with me rationally about what I needed to do next and sort of put some priorities in front of me. For instance, I was absolutely broke, and he encouraged me to borrow some money from the bank (which I did) so I could get my own apartment.

In the meantime, before I found my apartment (a period of about two to three weeks), I continued to live at Rich and Amy's. I felt completely out of place. As a result, I turned to those with whom I felt the most comfortable: Brian and Andy. I spent practically every evening with Brian. We'd go out to dinner and either to a movie or just walking around and looking for an apartment. He couldn't have been more understanding and helpful than if he were actually feeling what I felt. I also called on Andy, who was an absolute dream. He gave me the tenderness and caring that I thought Jason would but didn't. He helped me look for an apartment and offered to do absolutely anything for me. He asked nothing in return and demonstrated his feelings by being there when I needed him.

At first I didn't even want to be around the house when Rich and Amy were there (or at least awake). I didn't know what to say and felt ill at ease, so I stayed away as much as I could possibly arrange. As time passed, I began to peer into my mind and to think back over the past six months. I somehow seemed to have these revealing thoughts mostly when I was driving; I was doing a lot of that back and forth to San Francisco to see Brian. One of the thoughts I had was the feeling that Rich (perhaps Amy, too) expected me to always be one person, the same all the time. Perhaps this came because of some past conversation and/or actions, but it suddenly occurred to me that I always felt this with Rich. I'm not sure, but I think I could be a little bit more flexible with Amy. I have something of the same feeling about Brian. He always expects me to be just one Karen, when actually there are many Karens. I understand that there are certain background expectations all of us have regarding others; without them, we would have difficulty functioning. But there are other parts of me I'd like to explore and be. Somehow, I've allowed myself to present only one side. And I don't like the narrowness of that.

Upon further reflection, I discovered that I was extremely threatened by Rich's masculinity, intimidated by his big ego, penis, intellect, etcetera. This was especially in relation to my newfound bisexuality and the discovery of the masculine part

of *me*. I also came to realize that I really don't find Rich
sensuous or romantic. I think of him as too clinical, always
analyzing and dissecting feelings and actions. Now I must
hastily add that that's what makes Rich the person he is. His
kind of mind makes it possible for an individual to examine
himself, to make important discoveries. I understand that
perfectly, and I am grateful for the tiny bit that rubbed off
on me, but I still prefer a bit of mystery and a let's-not-
examine-it-if-it-just-feels-good attitude. Rich seemed never
to relax his thinking process to let that happen or be. I now
need to examine my own feelings and interpretation of mystery.

Toward the very end of January, I began to notice a
change in Amy. She seemed almost ecstatically happy, and
I began to notice a very small sliver of distance. Perhaps it
had been there all along since the split, but at this time, it was
becoming obvious to me. I somehow felt closer to her than
to Rich, even after we decided I'd leave. Perhaps she was just
covering up her feelings about me, or maybe I just wasn't
receiving signals. Anyway, as it got closer to the time when
I would be moving out, Amy became more friendly but in
a strange kind of way. I really don't understand it yet. Was
I projecting feelings, or were the vibrations as strong as they
felt? I at least had observed enough of these vibes to make
a note on scratch paper and put it in my journal, so I can't
be completely off base. The note specified the put-on friendli-
ness toward me and the harsh, forced laughter I've seen
before when she is embarrassed or doesn't know what to do
with the void in the conversation. My hand-written note
stuck in the journal doesn't specify any particular instance,
just the gesture and vibes themselves. These feelings still
remain today. Somehow she and I never did get it together.
We had the opportunity but never the time. Or so we
thought.

COMMENTARY:
The Human Dynamics and the Social Context

In the pages that follow, the editors offer some interpretation of Rich and Amy and Karen's six months together. We invite both a more careful look at the internal dynamics of their shared experience *and* some exploration of the relationship between this group marriage experiment and the larger social context in which it occurred. Because we see self, family, and society in an ongoing dialectical relationship, we believe that each kind of analysis is incomplete without the other.

The interpretation offered here is not the definitive one, nor is it entirely objective; our view of the matter clearly grows out of the particular themes and questions that presently intrigue us most. Because the diaries have more to say than any particular interpretation will bring into view, we wished to give readers access to them unprejudiced by commentary. However, our reflections might have some unique value because of our more careful reading of the journals, our conversations and correspondence with Amy and Rich and Karen, our knowledge of other similar experiments, and our familiarity with the pertinent sociological and psychological literature.

I

Reading these journals, you come to feel a tragic inevitability inherent in the unfolding of events. You see the seeds of difficulty from the beginning, some acknowledged as challenges, some pushed aside, some not consciously perceived by those involved. You read these accounts, at least the first time through, not as a report on group marriage as such but as the story of three individuals who, as one of them put it, got in over their heads.

But to learn from these records all they might teach us, it is necessary to shake off this sense of the inevitable and the feeling of sadness you are left with at the end. It is important to remember that although this account reads almost like fiction, where the pattern is determined by the esthetic imagination, the events narrated here happened to real people who live in a world where there is no such external ordering power. We need to enter into the most critical moments of their time together as moments that might have been lived through in different ways, might have led toward different futures; those moments must be seen as times of genuine choice. What happens between Amy and Rich and Karen happens in our world, at a particular moment in social history when the definition of family and the attitudes toward sexuality dominant in our society for most of this century have lost their taken-for-granted authority. *We* live in the same time, suffer the same pressures, share many of the same fantasies. Thus, we read their story as much for what it discloses about *us* as for what it reveals about Karen or Amy or Rich.

It is true that we learn from their story in much the same way that we learn from fiction: by having our lives expanded through imaginative participation in the lives of others.[1] Still, it is important that this story really happened. There are very few firsthand accounts of serious attempts at group marriage that convey the day-by-day feel of living together, reported honestly by the participants themselves from their different perspectives and revealing so much more than consciously intended.

The journals provide a very different view from that given by a clinical case study approach. Even when the psychologist recognizes the necessity of studying a whole family and studying it in its own home (as Jules Henry does[2]) his visit lasts only a week or two. Even when the sociologist presents his material almost entirely in the form of taped interviews (as Oscar Lewis does[3]) so that the words are those of the subjects themselves, the questions are the sociologist's, and he is responsible for editing and thus for interpreting. In both cases, the reader's knowledge of those being studied is filtered through the consciousness of an external observer, colored by his professional and personal biases. Even fictional accounts of experiments that are very similar to the one Rich and Amy and Karen undertook[4] suffer from being the fantasy of but one imagination, a fantasy not complicated by entanglement with competing fantasies or with the reality principle. But as each reader confronts these three journals directly, he must be his own interpreter and read in the light of his own fantasies and fears.

Rich and Amy and Karen had no models. There were no accounts of other group marriages from which they might have learned what to expect, what to watch out for, what to hope for. They knew one other threesome and also the participants in a four-person marriage, but their times with these others were given over to having fun together in an atmosphere of mutual (although mostly implicit) support. Shortly before Karen's departure, there was some talk of these ten people getting together much more self-consciously in an encounter group, but that project was conceived too late.

There were no models available because so few of those involved in experimental living arrangements are willing to expose themselves as these three people have. There are many more such explorations under way in ordinary suburban neighborhoods than most people would suspect, but the participants treasure their privacy, scrupulously avoiding the intrusions of clinical analysis and/or publicity. The few accounts of successful experiments that are available seem shallow compared with this narrative because they are without real crises, and therefore the participants are not forced to look at themselves and their relationships as closely. Similarly, there is little journal keeping during this group's most peaceful period. How much more often Rich and Karen write as their relationship becomes complicated and tense.

There is a related difficulty. Rich and Amy and Karen had no counselors, no one outside the marriage (friend or professional) to whom they felt ready to trust their confusions. Bob and Kathy might have been such friends, but they moved away. So might Jonathan and Cindy, but they were in Los Angeles and thus too far away. How unapt members of the helping professions are to be sympathetic to those engaged in deviant life-styles is suggested by the response of the psychiatrist Jason consulted.

Because these three people were willing to be more open, their story can serve as a model for others. If these accounts encourage others to explore and share their own fantasies, even if they know that they are not now ready to act these fantasies out (because of the level of their self-understanding or the state of their marriage or because there seem to be no other likely participants), they will through the fantasizing itself perhaps have been freed from their complacent, ready-made world. To imagine myself the wife called upon to share my bed with my husband and another woman night after night, to be expected to feel oneself a wholly equal partner in a relationship that also includes a legally married pair who have been living together for five years, to be a husband having to meet the emotional demands of two women simultaneously and without respite for six straight months—to become really immersed in such fantasies is to be changed. Such fantasizing calls our own attitudes toward monogamy, jealousy, and privacy into question. And if honestly pursued, such questioning may reveal that some shibboleths have more power in our lives than we had realized. By putting ourselves inside this story, we can understand our own hang-ups even when they are different from the ones that had the deepest hold on these particular individuals. By exploring their story, we may prepare ourselves to live out our own lives more imaginatively and more perceptively.

Such a reading is possible because these accounts, although full of numerous and greatly varied sexual involvements, are not pornography. Sexuality for these people does not mean exploitation or purely physical enjoyment. They see it, rather, as a power that pulls people together and separates them. As self-consciously sexually liberated people, these three try to speak of sex very matter-of-factly, very coolly. They would find it awkward to speak as Freud does of Eros, of sex in its mythical dimensions. Yet, clearly, what we have here is a focus, not on coitus, but on human relationships.

Indeed, there are surprisingly few detailed accounts of their lovemaking. Rich writes fairly often of how beautifully the three come to make love together, but he also notes how reticent and overgentle they all were with one another at first. Perhaps the most sexually stimulating accounts are the ones of the show-and-tell session in the camper, in which each showed how he or she masturbated and how they could give one another the fullest possible pleasure. Clearly, there is a genuine desire to help one another become better lovers, more free of inhibitions, more open to their own bisexuality, better able to cope with jealousy. Nevertheless, we cannot help but notice how little lovemaking there is among them for long periods of time. The reasons given are Rich's health, scheduling difficulties, the women's menstrual cycles. But these reasons never seem wholly adequate. Karen attributes much of the interpersonal tension to the lack of sexual intercourse, but the reverse may be as true.

Their account is not pornography, nor is it the account of a failure. It is important to Rich and Amy that we not see it as such. It is also important for us. They took their experiment and themselves very seriously. They understand themselves as examples of responsible deviance. That is precisely what gave them the strength to enter upon such an experiment, to emerge from it unhurt, and to be willing to share what appears to be a failure. In part, the decision to release the journals is obviously motivated by the hope of salvaging something. Yet, there is more to it than that. They see their time together, not as proving that such arrangements cannot work, but as presenting a history from which others might learn. Their story suggests that deviant experimentation will not work automatically, naturally, even for good, well-motivated, liberated people, but it also suggests that apparent failures will not destroy such people. Therefore, their account is not presented as the history of a failure, nor even as a guide that others might successfully follow by avoiding their pitfalls. The lesson is never that simple. This is just one story. Most such stories are written to prove one point or another: that such an experiment is an inevitable success or an inevitable failure or that this failure teaches a plan for success. This one simply says: "Here is how it was."

So let us look more closely at this how it was. This particular group marriage was initiated as a self-conscious experiment by two people confident of the strength of their marriage. Rich and Amy are intellectuals. Their professional concerns, an already tested commitment to personal exploration of sexual deviance, and a self-admitted curiosity encouraged them to undertake this particular experiment. These same factors undoubtedly helped them to stay with it when it became difficult and made them faithful and perceptive journal keepers. The invitation to Karen to live with them was not a casual decision. The relationship between Rich and Karen was a long-standing one, and although they had not seen each other in several years, they had remained in close touch. The general idea was one Rich and Amy had played with often. Karen's decision to leave her Texas lover and job made this seem the right time to act on it. There were many letters and tapes and telephone calls in which they discussed what their living together would mean and what shape it would take.

Amy and Rich had known each other for eight years and had been married for four of those years. They had a long experience of an open marriage and thus believed they had learned how to cope with all sorts of jealousy-provoking situations. However, they had not realized how thoroughly they had protected one another by their implicit agreement that there were no limits on sexual involvements with others as long as these were kept free of any emotional investment which might threaten the preeminence of their pair bond. This seems true despite their disclaimers that their extramarital relationships had often been anything but casual. Still, they developed deep trust of one another and a living arrangement that worked well for them. They were both at the thresholds of careers that they found stimulating and that they could share. For neither was the primary bond ever in question during even the most tumultuous periods of the group marriage. Their diaries report a few moments of tension and some occasional sexual dysfunction but no real difficulties between them. Rich seems to have been aware from the beginning of the problems that the long-established closeness between him and Amy might create for Karen, although Amy appeared confident that they had room for her at their center.

Karen's initial reasons for entering the group marriage were, of course, different. For her, it signified a new beginning. She seems to have had some rather naïve hopes of being able to leave the immediate past behind without having to integrate it. Her hopes were encouraged by her very deep trust of Rich and Amy, her memories of Rich as a good lover and friend, her idealized image of their marriage. She had no abstract interest in group marriage as a new form of family life and no investment in being innovative or deviant for its own sake. Her motives are very similar to those that might have propelled her into a conventional marriage.

At the beginning, all three seem to have shared some almost romantic hopes about what the group marriage would come to mean. Clearly, it was not understood as mostly a convenient living arrangement or mostly a way of providing a built-in orgy; each expressed expectations of participating in an intense and deeply intimate relationship likely to persist over a long period of time. Their plans to pool their financial resources and to prepare for careers that would mesh with one another symbolize this. Some male chauvinist elements are discernible in the way these plans were spelled out, but the seriousness of the intent to become one family must be acknowledged.

Yet, so many mutual expectations were never made explicit. Karen came to feel that she was involved in a game whose rules she learned only by making wrong moves. Perhaps none of them were enough aware of how much more demanding it is to live as one of a threesome than as one of a pair. There are twice as many crucial primary relationships for each participant to maintain, and it is important that all are in balance. It was Rich's understanding of this that underlay his oft-reiterated concern about the weakness of the bond between the two women. Multiple relationships also seem to call for more independence on the part of each participant because each will be left out of some important events and conversations. However, everything that happens between any two happens on stage, within view of the third's judgment and response. Amy had some preawareness of this; she hoped that in the threesome, she would come "out to stay." She looked forward to an openness and transparency between them that she had never before known. Rich expected that a third person might often provide sympathetic but usefully critical feedback. As it turned out, Amy was sometimes able to serve helpfully as a mediator when things became tense between Rich and Karen. But much of the time, the complexities of the many-vectored relationships seemed overwhelming.

The group marriage was clearly Rich's project. Karen had some real basis for wondering, as she did toward the end, whether Amy had ever really wanted it or had just gone along with him. Rich is the one with the most curiosity and imagination and also the strongest commitment to sexual deviance and social change. He is also clearly the one at the center of the threesome, as symbolized by their usual way of sleeping with him in the middle, especially during the first few months. The women hardly knew one another when Karen appeared at the home of Rich's parents, and even after months of living together, they continued to relate to one another *through* him. Each had a lot to contend with. Amy had to make room for another woman, not just at the periphery of her marriage, but at its very center; Karen had to find her place in relation to a strong ongoing twosome. But the burden of initiative and insight remained on Rich, as he seems to have assumed it would.

The journals, too, are really his project. It is his persistence that keeps Amy and Karen writing. If we are sometimes put off by his entries, we should remember that. His entries attempt to set their experiment in a wider sociological and philosophical context. Consequently, his journal seems the least personally revealing; he rarely speaks of his own pains or confusions except on those occasions when he analyzes his jealousy, almost as though it were another's. He is aware of this tendency toward abstraction and knows that it can serve as a defense mechanism, knows that by talking analytically about what is happening, he can duck personal confession. But that *is* Rich; he really *does* cope with his hard times by objectifying them. That he is like this is part of the drama, not digression, as is particularly evident after it is all over. Rich writes often in his journal at that juncture, but rarely to display his own feelings or probe his own responsibility. Mostly, he rehearses the social significance of experiments like theirs.

Rich is also the one most aware of the difficulty of conveying the subtleties of feelings and interpersonal exchange. Both women have high regard for his intelligence and encourage him in just such philosophizing and moralizing. They truly believe he sees more clearly than they, more deeply and more honestly, and respect his forcing them to be more conscious. Often, Rich's comments (defense maneuvers though they may be) are pertinent to a broader understanding of what is going on. His commitment to the journal project keeps him faithfully writing. Without him, we would have almost no chronicle of the time between the return from the vacation trip to Mexico and the time in early fall when the atmosphere is already thick with turmoil, distrust, and confusion. Rich's concern that their living together be a highly self-conscious enterprise helps to explain how often the individual accounts seem to give very similar interpretations of a particular event. He insists that crises be talked through, that they strive for group consensus.

Amy's and Karen's journals are very different. Amy starts out with enthusiasm for the new project she and Rich have embarked on, glad to be helping by putting into her diary immediate and beautifully honest accounts of her response to what is happening. But as things get rough, her entries become less and less frequent, as though she no longer feels herself to be a primary actor in the unfolding story. The drama is being enacted between Rich and Karen. Between Karen and Amy, there is only the heavy weight of an OK relationship that never grows, as symbolized by their never growing closer sexually. Her puzzlement at the charged tension between Rich and Karen—so different from her own relationship with him—and at Rich's bewitchment by it, lead to her one uncharacteristic outburst, reported only by Karen: "You must love Karen more than me." She clearly becomes exhausted by the mediating role imposed upon her but is certain all along of the strength and permanence of her own relationship with Rich.

Karen at first resists writing a journal. This annoys Rich, who perceives it as a sign of her not sharing his values and priorities and of not being fully committed to the group marriage. For her, it may have been a way of saying that she wanted to be included in the marriage *as herself,* that she felt in herself some resistance to being considered a subject in an experiment, although she voices this only much, much later. Because she begins her journal late, her first entries are musings over the events of several weeks at a time. She integrates experiences very differently from Rich: not by way of abstraction, but by retrospectively imposing on them a unifying feeling tone. Things stay with her, as her final entries testify. She has few techniques for bringing feelings to a place where she can free herself from them; thus, she seems to move mostly in response to unconscious feeling and to be little able to respond to Rich's plea that she become more conscious.

Initially, she seems to be writing for Rich. There is never much sense that she is writing for a public. Her later entries suggest that she is using the journal to sort through and get hold of her own responses. She is perhaps the one whose journal best conveys *her* feelings. She is also the one who tries least to understand the feelings of the other two.

Rich's highly conscious intellectual approach to the group marriage puts him in charge, makes the whole thing *his* experiment. It is undeniable that for both Amy and Karen, it seemed natural to have Rich dominate. They do not feel exploited by this, as a self-conscious feminist would. Rich, too, seems largely unconscious of any male chauvinism. It is displayed, not so much in his repeated references to the two women as "the girls," but rather in his assumption throughout that he is the one with the most insight and strength, the least inhibited, the least conventional.

The women comply with the directive. They tend to accept Rich's interpretations, to adopt his vocabulary, to internalize his vision of their insecurity. This is especially true of Amy, who is grateful to Rich for having helped her to grow, open up, "come out to play" during the years they have lived together. During the acid trip she and Rich take together in late December (when she sees him as the central power source in his study-become-energy-cell), the awe she feels is simply a dramatized version of her everyday relation to him.

Karen, too, accepts Rich's analyses and sees her low self-esteem and lack of self-confidence as a kind of bond with Amy. Karen's insecurities were manifested before she came to live with Rich and Amy by her inability to break away from her lover, Brian. They are also evident in her return to him after she leaves Rich and Amy. They are expressed in how easily she is provoked to jealousy by Amy's relationship with Joyce and Rich's with Maggie. Karen suffers from headaches and menstrual cramps. She manifests some sexual dysfunction—some difficulty in having orgasms, a deep reluctance to take initiative, a fear of inadequate response if

Amy were to make love to her. Whenever she moves to overcome such insecurity, Rich seems to want to take credit for the move; it is inspired by him, is somehow his achievement. It is noteworthy that it never seems to occur to Rich that women as a group in our culture have problems with low self-esteem—nor that he may be a contributor to their neurosis.

But Rich, too, has his insecurities, even though he has developed better coping mechanisms and seems very secure to those close to him. He expresses an almost pathological fear of loneliness, and both women know there is something false in his assumption that their need for moments of solitude always represents escapist withdrawal. Despite his wish that it were otherwise, Rich still expresses a lot of sexual jealousy, especially with respect to Karen. This jealousy also appears to underlie his habit of "restaking his claim" whenever Karen or Amy have made love with someone else. His health and the continuing toll of the earlier skiing accident are constant concerns. Several times, he voices feelings of sexual inadequacy even though he clearly has quite a few sexual partners. But the only inadequacy he ever explicitly admits to is his inability to help Karen with *her* insecurity.

For all his implicit chauvinism, Rich gives verbal support to women's liberation. He is clearly proud of Amy's professional accomplishments, although he tends to speak of them as *his* creation, his gift. This Pygmalion complex comes out even more vividly with respect to Karen, whom he clearly wants to feel he has liberated. *He* decides she should go to school; *he* wants her to prepare herself to be a colleague on *his* projects. It seems pertinent in this connection to note that when Karen leaves to return to her old job and to at least some degree of involvement with her old lover, it is as though —unsatisfying as these might be—they were *hers* in a way that the life Rich programmed for her never really was. She resists his attempts to mold her more than Amy seems to have done. Karen does so partly out of a kind of cowardice but perhaps also out of an instinctive and necessary need for *self*-protection.

Karen's resistance suggests that she and Amy are less alike than all three seem to have assumed at the beginning. This seems to have been an important myth, one suggested at the beginning by discovering a similarity of taste in towels and china. Rich's plans for Karen seem to represent an expectation of making her another Amy: a blonder, more buxom version. And Amy speaks of Karen as a "true sister," another internal half. One of the differences, as her greater resistance to Rich's programming may imply, is that Karen seems to have a stronger (although unconscious and undeveloped) "masculine" side. It is a side that is revealed in the drug trips and in the shape of the only two sexual encounters between her and Amy in both of which she takes the active, initiating role.

Each woman began with hopes of establishing with the other a deep friendship such as neither had experienced with another woman. Each had had some lesbian experience, and it seemed almost taken for granted that they would become lovers. Yet, nothing substantial ever happened, although they seem to have enjoyed making love together with Rich. To some degree, their becoming lovers was part of Rich's program. Clearly, he was the one most conscious of how little their relationship was growing, how little they shared emotionally. And it was Rich who saw their sexual reticence with each other as a sign of this. Yet, the homosexual bond was something the women also wanted. Amy's first journal entries express her longing to be as important to Karen as Rich is, as able to give Karen sexual fulfillment. Some of this may have been a disguise for a more conventional jealousy, but some of it seems to be authentic. There can be little question of the authenticity of Karen's jealousy of Joyce, Amy's first female lover. At the very end, after Christmas, Karen comes to Amy and initiates a sexual encounter with her, as if she can relate *directly* to Amy only after her relationship with Rich is out of the way. They make love at the beginning, when they are not yet with Rich, and at the end. That second lovemaking, like Rich's Christmas roses, seems, not a new beginning, but the closing of a circle.

The esthetic patterning of these repetitions is eerie: the roses, the lovemaking between Karen and Amy, Karen's return to Brian and her old job. Furthermore, the shape of their six months together seems to fall naturally into a five-act development:

1. The period from the arrival in Palo Alto until the return from Mexico and the camping trip was a honeymoon, colored by a sense of beginning and anticipation. In retrospect, some seeds of discord are discernible even then. But, clearly, many different futures might have emerged from this beginning.

2. The time between the return from the vacation and the beginning of the busy fall term is a period about which the journals tell little. Only Rich was writing regularly. However, he and Amy (in her later attempt to reconstruct the stages they have passed through) see this as a time of peaceful consolidation, when all three felt at home in their new arrangement.

3. The real testing time occurred from late September until Thanksgiving, a time whose beginning was marked by Karen's getting involved with Andy and by her first LSD trip. During that trip, she revealed for the first time some of her hostility toward Rich. Such a time of testing was inevitable. It is something any enduring, growing relationship must suffer through. There were many sources of tension: the pressure of outside responsibilities, the pull of other sexual involvements, different responses to one another's friends, different attitudes toward money, different priorities with respect to time, different ways of responding to conflict. Throughout this period, Rich kept thinking that they were succeeding in handling the tensions better than do most marital partners. Perhaps no one took the strains seriously

enough; perhaps they lacked the necessary time or energy; maybe they had thought it would be easier. Two had made it work. It seemed as though including another would be quite natural.

4. The climax came between Thanksgiving and New Year's. The breakup was prefigured in the Thanksgiving weekend acid trip but was not wholly acknowledged for another month.

5. Finally, there was the period of disentanglement, physically and psychically.

This articulation of the stages may help to reveal a progression, may give a sense of what might have been different for these three or what might be different for another group. Obviously, it is an artificial demarcation, but of a kind we all engage in. We all choose particular episodes as metaphors, as marking-off points, in order to make sense of our experiences. Clearly, a different interpreter might choose different symbols, draw different lines.

Throughout all five stages, an inescapable fact was the continuing strength of the relationship between Rich and Amy. In a sense, of course, this was an asset. It was this durability that had made them feel ready to take on the group marriage, to invite Karen to join them. It became a liability, however, because Karen never did come to feel herself an equal partner. In fact, she came to see herself as a drag, as holding them back. It was not only that they had been together longer but also that too much was preset. The shape of the marriage had already been worked out between Rich and Amy. They were ready to expand it but not to redefine it.

There were many aspects of Rich and Amy's life with which Karen remained uncomfortable. The same interest in sexual liberation and deviance that had made Rich and Amy open to establishing a group marriage had led them to become at least peripherally involved in the swinging scene. The nudity, the casual sex, the group drug trips, all that characterized the parties to which they took Karen, continually made her feel out of place. She also felt awkward with most of their friends except the couple from Los Angeles and the couple who moved away. This awkwardness was then reflected in Amy and Rich's hesitancy in seeing much of their own close friends. In fact, a theme to which each returns is the difficulty of finding friends all three enjoy. The ad in the underground newspaper is evidence of this. They clearly feel socially isolated because of their threesome and are very self-conscious about their deviance. They like to feel they are setting an example for others. They have a strong sense of identification with the only other threesome they know.

Another problem of which they are all very conscious is that of overscheduling. So often, one or another will write that there is no time for relaxation, for quiet times together, for fun. This is especially so for Amy, who has to go out every day, who begins at this time to feel "left out" of much that happens between Rich and Karen. "No time" or "bad timing" are recurrent explanations offered when things don't go well.

The time pressure is directly related to the financial situation; Amy assumes a heavy teaching schedule because of their need for money. (It is obviously easier if you are as rich as Robert Rimmer's fictional experimenters tend to be.) Rich is ambivalent about money. There are clearly things that are more important to him; he evinces some deeply felt snobbery with respect to the country club set (with which he may identify Amy's family). But he is no hippie. He is proud of his comfortable home and the sensuous atmosphere created by its sheepskin rug and soft carpets, fur chair and good music. He is conscious from the beginning of not being able to provide for Karen the luxuries a Jason could; he knows that during the fall Karen comes to resent that there is never money or time for "fun" things like the theater and expensive restaurants. Still, Rich wants very much to handle their financial affairs in a way which will symbolize that they are one family, living out of one pot. He wants Karen to go to school and help with the house and his research rather than get a job. Perhaps she might have been happier and had a greater sense of self and independence if she had had a job. But she never says so.

A source of tension they were all much more conscious of was their various sexual involvements with persons beyond the threesome. They had recognized how important it was during the honeymoon period to focus on the relationships among the three of them. Karen saw Jason when he appeared, much too soon, but was clearly relieved to have him leave. During this time, Rich self-consciously and uncharacteristically abstained from getting involved with several women with whom it would ordinarily have seemed pleasant and natural to have sex. Perhaps the focus time was too short; perhaps they did not think ahead clearly enough about what outside involvements would be appropriate. In any case, they didn't seem prepared to handle it when both Rich and Karen got involved at the onset of stage three.

For Rich, it was a question of returning to a familiar pattern, one that he and Amy had long since accommodated themselves to: a pattern of having sexually involved relationships with several women, none threatening, none compulsive. Karen was often jealous but understood this as a sign of her own insecurity and lack of self-confidence. But the incident that really upset her occurred when she felt she had terminated her relationship with Jason and defused the relationship with Andy because of her concern for her relationship with Rich only to come home to find that he was with the woman she most resented.

There was more involved in Karen's outside relationships than in Rich's, as he and Amy were quick to sense. There were grounds for Amy's hurt and Rich's jealousy but also for Karen's reaching out for such involvements. Amy had foreseen from the beginning Karen's wish for a primary relationship and how this might show itself were she not to feel wholly included in the new family. Long before Karen was conscious of not feeling herself a full member, there was that in her which reached for a relationship outside the group to give her a kind of balance. Rich was terribly jealous of Karen, especially of her involvement with Andy. He didn't want to be but was, nevertheless. He felt that Karen's going out with several different men and several times a week (just when he and Amy were most deeply caught up in their teaching and writing responsibilities) was a betrayal of the group marriage. Karen's involvements were more threatening than Amy's had ever been because they seemed to express a deeper need, a search for "her own man."

All this was difficult for Amy because she had no other sexual relationships during this time except the one with Joyce, which was so problematic for Karen. Yet, she was called upon to play mediator between Karen and Rich as they were working through their jealousies and to help and support each.

As things became tense between Rich and Karen, he writes that it sometimes seems she doesn't know how to love or to let another love her. At the very beginning, when Karen had told Rich that the psychiatrist Jason consulted had said the same thing, Rich had dismissed it as pernicious and prejudiced. Yet, he eventually came to explain her reaching out to others in the same language. This explanation is too simple, although Rich's adoption of it gives it much power in shaping the subsequent unfolding of events and makes it easy to lay the primary responsibility for the breakup of the group marriage on Karen—on how Karen *is* in some given, eternal way—rather than on specific deeds, events, and responses. It *is* true that Karen is the most self-centered of the three. Perhaps because there are fewer filters between her and her feelings, she seems more honest. Perhaps because she doesn't have a partner to whom she can trust herself completely (as Rich and Amy can with one another), there is a part of Karen that knows, long before she writes it in December, that "you make it on your own, baby, or not at all."

At the beginning, she had hoped it might be otherwise. All three had had such romantic expectations, although Rich, when playing with the idea of challenging the state's bigamy statutes, had, in a sort of knock-on-wood gesture, acknowledged the possibility of failure. Most of the causes for the eventual breakup lay quite deep: in insecurities and mistrust, in the imbalances between the strength of the relationship between Rich and Amy on the one hand and their relationship with Karen on the other, in differences in long-established styles of response to tension, in the demanding living situation. But some causes seemed to be functions of sheer chance and bad timing. These came to symbolize the others, perhaps because it is easier to isolate and analyze the extraordinary moment than the everyday routine patterns of relating. Karen's spending time with Jason during the first week of the group marriage and Rich's having sex with Maggie on the very night Karen felt she had made some decisive breaks with Jason and Andy came to be read as irredeemable betrayals. Nevertheless, it is important to recognize that the difficulties were really more pervasive, more structural.

At least two acid trips came to have the same symbolic power. Rich and Amy had been using LSD for some time as part of a conscious therapeutic program to work on getting past some of their fears and hostilities, as well as occasionally taking very small quantities to enhance their appreciation of music, visual stimuli, and sex. Karen had had almost no experience with drugs, but after listening to Amy and Rich talk of their experiences, reading some books they suggested, and being around while others were tripping, she felt ready to try it herself. Her first trip took place in late September; it freed her to express quite directly some of her latent hostilities toward Rich and brought her into touch with her own "masculinity." At the time, she felt it to have been "good" but "heavy": the first real confrontation with Rich and the discovery of the underlying deep commitment between them. But Amy was alienated by Karen's attack on Rich, and all three in retrospect came to look upon this trip as marking the beginning of the period of conflict and tension. During Karen's second trip, in late November, Rich seems to have pushed the focus onto the emotional distance between her and Amy. Again, it was a tense experience, full of conflict, but one that Karen felt had been therapeutic, one that she believed they should repeat. Once again, in retrospect, the meaning seemed to change. This came to be seen as the occasion when the distance between Karen and both of the other two had inescapably revealed itself. Both drug trips then were occasions for the crystallization and condensation of everything else that was going wrong.

From late September on, each week seemed to bring a new conflict into view between Rich and Karen. Amy writes on October 18: "Everything has been so *heavy.*" In fact, it seems amazing that, despite this recurring tension, the three stayed together for another three months. Several times during this second half of their time together, Karen wonders whether she really belongs, and Amy wonders if she and Rich have taken on more than they can handle. The Thanksgiving weekend drug trip signals the coming of the end; the dismal attempt to celebrate Christmas together heralds its arrival.

Each of them responds to the ending in a different and characteristic way. Amy seems mostly to have felt relief. She also felt the ending had happened without her really being part of it. Her presence is felt less and less as the story unfolds. She had started out with such high expectations, but as things became difficult, she found a way of withdrawing into her work, a withdrawal probably made possible by her conviction that there was nothing really at stake for her, that her marriage was secure in any event. Neither Rich nor Amy seem to have been seriously hurt by the outcome. Nor were they deeply touched or transformed by it, although of course they were not immune to the pain and trauma inherent in the ending. The same defenses that protected them from hurt protected them from transformation. All three come to recognize how much easier (and thus, of course, less challenging) a twosome is than a threesome; Karen discovers in herself the same reaching for that kind of security that we see in Rich and Amy. Rich tended to escape confronting the experience directly on the level of feeling by examining it from a sociodynamic perspective. He was also able to put most of the blame on Karen or on Karen and Amy's failure to develop their relationship.

Karen internalized this notion that the primary responsibility for the breakdown lay with her, her insecurities, her immaturity, her selfishness. She persists in her somewhat romantic view of the bond between Rich and Amy; she is more in touch now with its peculiarities but deeply impressed by how well it works for them. She was also clearly the one least protected against the failure, the least personally secure, the one left on her own when it was all over. In March, it still hurts for her.

We might wish that all three had been less ready to rely on Karen's insecurity as the explanation for what happened. That seems both too easy and too fatalistic. They might instead have sought for specific situations to which they could have responded differently. They might have tried to be more conscious of the feelings of the others involved, more aware of likely repercussions. Group marriage seems to demand a high consciousness of options, of the many different ways of responding to the possibilities of a particular moment. It calls for a deliberate choice among these options on the basis of one's sense of likely consequences. It also seems to demand the courage to try again, to try something different and perhaps more risky, less familiar, when one response does not work very well. In a sense, this threesome was plagued by having too many options. There were almost no hard-and-fast rules about outside involvements or the other things that became focuses of tension. Such openness and freedom call for great sensitivity and imagination and the ability to draw boundaries for oneself.

Amy saw at the beginning that a group marriage can

provide a unique opportunity for encouraging honesty and trust and personal growth. No doubt it can. But the choice of the deviant path guarantees neither failure nor success. This does not mean that Karen and Rich and Amy would have had to be wholly secure, mature, integrated individuals for their threesome to have worked better than it did; rather, it means that they seem not to have been aware ahead of time of how much energy and imagination and hope would be required. But we, with their accounts in hand, may be able to discern more about their time together than they did and thus to see new possibilities inherent in our own stories.

II

The purpose of this book is to provide a close look at one well-documented experiment with an alternative to the traditional family. Our understanding of the group marriage described here and of other new life-style options will be served by an awareness of the social context in which it was constructed and by an exploration of some of the interconnections that link certain key culturally resonant phenomena of the past decade. It is, of course, impossible to do justice to the complexities of the period in a few pages, but it would be irresponsible to ignore the cultural milieu that supplied some of the boundaries within which Karen and Amy and Rich worked and played.

Human life as we know it is impossible without institutions. The word *institution* refers to any pattern of human arrangements that helps give order to human conduct; its use should not be restricted to highly visible buildings and bureaucracies. The Department of Defense and the San Diego Zoo are institutions, but so are our courtship patterns, family structures, party etiquette, and even the language we speak.

Doubts about the value of existing institutions and experimentation with new institutional forms appear together in history. Turbulent times are strange mixtures of dissatisfaction and hope, of angry resentment and feverish reconstruction. Such an unstable blend of hostility toward the status quo and high expectations for this or that reformist or revolutionary future has been an important part of the American experience, especially for the last dozen years or so. The unprecedented affluence of the period since World War II has made it possible for the middle-class young to extend their adolescence considerably, to increase substantially the number of years spent reading; traveling; experimenting; interacting with peers, teachers, and gurus; and dreaming. University communities have become worldview marketplaces where plans of salvation, implicit and explicit, are propounded, picked apart, adopted, and discarded.

The media brought the dark side of the American experience to the attention of the nation's youth. In response, they formed various movements that sought to correct injustice and to improve the quality of life. The new crusaders listed among their enemies racism, poverty, corporate greed, irrelevant religious institutions, and a war in Asia. They envisioned a fundamental transformation of the society; they expected to prevail. But gradually, as the sixties wore on, something went wrong. Some of the reformers said that the large institutions—the spheres of the political, the economic, and the religious—could not be redeemed. Others said they were not *worth* redeeming. Still others merely became tired or distracted. Much of the energy that had been invested in political activism was redirected into more personal versions of the quest for meaning: drug mysticism, Eastern religions, the occult. Much of the remaining concern for social change was focused closer to home: on the schools and especially on the families, traditional and experimental, in which the young found themselves. There is evidence to suggest that failure to change the macrostructure has contributed to this redirection of reformist zeal into the transformation of the nearer world of the family. In the paragraphs that follow, we shall explore the extent to which *public* interest in and *experimentation with a whole host of alternative forms of intimate relationships is continuous with earlier efforts to change larger institutions.*

The process by which sixties activism has been transmuted into various forms of seventies interiorism is part of a much larger transformation that had its beginning in the Industrial Revolution. As technology develops, each generation of workers, office personnel, technicians, and managers is more specialized than the one before. The results are a loss of pride in workmanship and a loss of a sense of a meaningful whole.

In Western industrial society, work has become a problem because most people still subscribe to the notion that work ought to be meaningful, but the demands of the industrial system are such that most jobs are boring, repetitive, segmented, and unfulfilling. Put simply, we *expect* to find meaning in our work, but we don't.

When work is devalued by the routinization that modern industry and commerce demand, it can no longer give meaning to the lives of individuals. *Public life* (those activities given shape by occupation) is seen as unsatisfactory, and so, in compensation, one turns one's attention to the *private sphere* (that aspect of life which occurs apart from the world of work). The individual whose public life is overdirected by the routines of production and bureaucracy turns inward to home life and leisure and to a personalized version of the quest for meaning.

Marriage and family life, then, become a prime location of the private business of meaning making. At home, the individual has the apparent power to fashion a world that will reflect personal values and may do so without clashing with the major social, economic, and political institutions of the larger society. On the job, I may be an insignificant component of an unfeeling machine, but at home, I am the boss. At home, I am *somebody.*[5]

All social activity has a personal dimension. Individuals are not only objects being moved by social forces; they are also subjects, actors and reactors with feelings and needs. And one very pervasive personal need, pertinent here, is the need to know that things have changed because one has acted, that one has the power to modify one's environment, natural and human.

The would-be social reformer is no different from anyone else. He craves evidence that his efforts have had some impact. And he is often impatient; he needs the feedback that affords rather immediate reinforcement.

Postwar affluence and the education, the leisure, and the media-fed awareness of social failures which that affluence has facilitated have democratized the prerogatives of the social critic and the architect of change. Where once there stood a handful of intellectuals, artists, and political leaders modestly sanding the rough corners of the societal edifice, the sixties gave us millions of overeducated young people striving in diverse ways to raze that structure and build another in its place.

In time, however, the testimony of the same media that had originally inspired them convinced the young reformers that they were not effective. Racism, poverty, and war rumbled on, and the major institutions of American society held their own.

If one needs to see oneself as an effective agent (as, we would submit, all human beings do), *and if* certain individuals are optimistic about solving major social problems (as seems to have been true of many young people in the sixties), *and if* those problems are resistant to quick and complete solution (as recent experience suggests they are), *then* we should not be surprised to discover that the energies of the would-be reformers are redirected toward an institutional sphere more susceptible to change and more apt to give evidence that it is changing: namely, the family. To extend this reconstruction metaphor: Young reformers who were dissatisfied with their ability to alter substantially the living room, the dining room, and the kitchen are now trying to remake the bedroom and the nursery.

In this endeavor, in contrast with political activity, the reformer is more likely to get the reassuring feedback he craves. Whereas other major institutions are organized from the top in such a way that their local manifestations resist change initiated from the grass-roots level, the broad institution called the American family is perhaps better understood as the sum of its parts. If an individual self-consciously alters his own living arrangement, he immediately sees concrete evidence that things have changed because he has acted *and* he can feel, if he so chooses, that he has made a small but very real change in that larger reality, the American family.

To sum up: The frustrations that adults meet in the world of work drive them to look for meaning in the family setting. This may or may not involve alteration of the orthodox family form. The frustrations that many adolescents and young adults feel as they contemplate their social, political, and economic impotence drive them to experiment with alternatives to the traditional family. In both situations, the quest for meaning has been brought home.

There are three principal loci for the reinvestment of energy that formerly was given to political activism: education reform; mysticism, the inner trip mediated either by drugs or by Eastern religious traditions; and interest in and experimentation with alternative forms of intimate association.

Of these three avenues, it is probably fair to say that education reform is the most political, but even the new mysticism may be interpreted as a response to earlier failures in the political realm. If the Kingdom cannot be established on earth, it will be found within.

It is not our intention to suggest that such diverse behaviors as political activism and devotion to Eastern religions ought to be lumped together or seen as different loci for the investment of some generalized élan vital. Zen is very different from antiwar politics. But there are continuities between such phenomena that ought not to be overlooked. Sociologists Robert Wuthnow and Charles Glock found that 60 percent of a sample of young devotees of Eastern religions but only 14 percent of conventionally religious youth think the United States is a sick society. These researchers conclude: "Religious defection and experimentation with new religious forms is part of a broader disillusionment with established society."[6]

The third route, experimentation with alternative forms of intimate association, seems for some to combine social-political and personal concerns. But this third route is really a multitude of paths. Recent experimentation with modifications of the family constitutes a *spectrum* of responses, a vast variety of approaches running the gamut from gentle tinkering to major surgery.

Radical experiments with alternative forms stand in a certain continuity with much less drastic attempts to modify and improve family life. The desire to enrich and revitalize more or less conventional marriages is widespread in the United States, and the media and the professions stand ready to assist. Books, magazines, and TV programs explore the ways in which family life is changing. They offer suggestions on how to have bigger and better orgasms, how to fight fair with one's spouse, how to be an effective parent, and so on. Psychotherapists, encounter group leaders, sex counselors, and clergymen advertise their readiness to help improve the quality of life in the intimate sphere. The popularity of a book like *Open Marriage,* by Nena and George O'Neill, and the recent formation of an organization such as the Association of Couples for Marriage Enrichment (ACME) remind us that most people who desire more meaningful intimate relationships do not opt for major modifications to conventional marriage. But such radical alternatives as group marriage, sexually open marriage, and swinging, are in part explained as alternative responses to the same impulses that inspire various marriage-enrichment approaches.

Communal living arrangements of various sorts differ from the marriage-enrichment approach in that they involve the self-conscious formation of households or communities of three or more adults who view themselves as linked together in some kind of partnership. A group marriage is one kind of communal living experience; not all communes are marked by nontraditional sexual arrangements.

Communes come in all sizes and styles.[7] The group marriage that this volume describes consisted of three people. The population of Twin Oaks, a Virginia commune based on B. F. Skinner's utopian novel *Walden Two,* stands between thirty and forty. Some communities are much larger. The setting may be rural, suburban, or urban. The participants may be poor or affluent. Some groups are organized around shared commitment to some creed or group goal; others lack such a center.

People go into cooperative living arrangements for many different reasons. Some are drawn primarily by economic benefits; others, by a strong desire for sexual variety. Some, like Rich, simply find themselves "in love" with more than one other person. Still others are moved by their perception of the needs of their children or to compensate for their own childlessness.

It is the testimony of his journal that Rich tried group marriage at least in part because of his ideological commitments and because of his need to see himself as the self-conscious creator of an alternative institution. The group marriage was for him an exercise in meaning making, a means of substantially altering his immediate context and, perhaps, catalyzing other changes beyond the walls of his home. Rich works in the spirit of the epigram from Paul

Goodman that hangs over his desk: "If there is no community for you, young man, young man, make it yourself." Rich understands the group marriage as a response both to personal needs and to the inadequacies of the larger society. In this connection, he has written:

> Our experiment in social deviance is justified, I feel, by the fact that the rest of the world has gone mad, killing, plundering, wrecking the earth for generations to come, perhaps permanently. Marriage and family life is a combination of a joke and a tragic incident for an ever-increasing number of persons. Love does not easily thrive in contemporary American society, built as it is on exploitation, waste, and aggressive competitiveness.... Amy and Karen and I are feeling our way to one type of private answer.
>
> Change must come if we are to move away from this collective madness. But the revolution, if there is to be one, begins, not merely at home, but in one's own heart and mind.... Any genuine and significant change must affect our *basic institutions,* our *fundamental values.* It must be a revolution in individual consciousness.

The careful reader will have found other expressions of these sentiments in Rich's journal.

Rich, it should be noted, has no history as a political activist. His political views may be classified as liberal to radical, but he has not given much energy to electoral politics, nor did he participate in the street demonstrations of the last decade. He has chosen a more contemplative, more intellectual route, but he wants to see the work he does in his study and the experiment he conducts in his home as political activities.

Such an attitude is not uncommon. Many of the communards and group marrieds we have interviewed and about whom we have read see their attempts to create new forms as political acts or as substitutes for more traditional political acts. For example, an article about the Twin Oaks commune includes these capsule biographies of two key members of the community:

> *Brian.* Dropped out of a large Southern university. Active civil rights protester who lost faith in the efficacy of demonstrations. Disgruntled over the lack of "postrevolutionary thinking" in political groups. A student of utopian literature. . . .
> *Dwight.* . . . Joined the community for almost purely idealistic reasons. Philosophy graduate student at a Midwestern university. Believed that the Good Life should be set up in miniature. Then as its appeal became obvious to people, the idea would simply grow.[8]

Amy manifests some utopian-political concern but not nearly so much as Rich. She seems to view their three-adult household primarily as a practical solution to problems of overwork and as an easy way of adding emotional richness to her life. Also, in her self-sketch, Amy reports that Rich has a higher sex drive than she and that she anticipated that with Karen around, Rich's needs would be met without Amy having to make love more than she desired.

Karen, in striking contrast to Rich, comes to the experiment with no abstract commitment to the construction of a utopia. Rather, she seems to have come to the group marriage out of a simple desire for intimate relationships and the security of a supportive household. In her self-sketch, Karen offers this simple response to the question: Why go into a group marriage? "Why does *anyone* want to get married? For love, for companionship, for sharing. Well, all these still apply; they're simply expanded." Karen is moved by needs not very different from those that lead others to enter conventional marriage. Of course, Karen differs from most people in being sufficiently uninhibited to seek the satisfaction of her needs in a nonconventional setting, but she does not share Rich's urge to reinvent the family and to change the world.

Some persons who join communes or experiment with group marriage move confidently from their strengths, seeking to add another dimension to a life that is already going well. Others rush desperately from their inadequacies, seeking utopian deliverance from dysfunctional pair bonds and personal failures. Again, one notes an imbalance in the group described in these journals. Rich and Amy had a strong, synergistic marriage. Karen was alone, having just broken off an unsatisfactory relationship with another man. Her need for the group marriage was much different from theirs, although there is little evidence that any of them was conscious of this at the beginning.

Some communes prohibit forms of sexual activity that are tolerated or encouraged in the larger society; total abstinence from sex is required in some religious communities. In some other groups, the erotic activity is governed by the same rules that obtain in the society outside: The marital bond is respected, and adulteries are met with some form of negative sanction. In still other communes, some more liberal set of sexual values and expectations is at work. In communal situations, toleration of premarital sex is quite common; toleration of sex outside of recognized pair bonds, although less common, is also found.

It is important to note that some communities have very liberal attitudes regarding the sexual experiences of members with persons from *outside* the living group but discourage or prohibit sexual activity outside of pair bonds *between* members of their group. Such restrictions are often seen as functional for the survival and smooth operation of the community. They may be part of the group's expectations from the beginning, or they may arise in response to some crisis situation.

Their journals suggest that Rich and Amy and Karen expected that sexual energy would (and ought to) flow in every conceivable direction among them *and* that each of them was also free to have sexual experiences outside their family circle. In time, the inability of the two women to form an ongoing homoerotic liaison and certain jealousies and misunderstandings in connection with the outside sexual interests and activities of all three became problematic. These strains seem to have contributed to the dissolution of the group.

Social institutions exist to reduce the total number of options that confront the individual, to reduce them from the infinite to the manageable. Monogamous marriage, for example, resolves the question: With whom shall I have sexual intercourse? It declares as taboo sexual interaction with any person other than one's spouse. A commitment to monogamous marriage, then, simplifies life; it delivers one from the trauma of decision.

When one devises an alternative to an existing institution, that alternative, like the pattern it replaces, must draw boundaries, devise rules, and set limits. Even if the new way allows greater latitude than did the old, it still limits the number of options. It still restricts; it still excludes. It is important to see experimental systems as new institutions, as patterns of order, not as the end of institutions and the absence of order.

Rich and Amy and Karen's experiment, although it departs substantially from the family form prevalent in this society, should not be dismissed as the antithesis of order. There are limits and restraints in their alternative to monogamy. You may come to feel that they drew their boundaries inappropriately, but it is important to see that theirs is an alternative pattern rather than an absence of pattern.

At a time when the nuclear family has lost its taken-for-granted authority for many people, such alternate orders are especially important. The creators of such orders can be seen as pioneers of a sort; the deviant can be one from whose exploratory journey we can learn. The journals opened here to public scrutiny, enable us to look over the shoulders of three persons who set out on an uncharted way. They record successes and failures from which we can learn, and they challenge us to participate in the same quest for meaning. They invite us to name the boundaries and constraints that seem appropriate to viable patterns of intimate association.

Notes on Commentary

[1]For a discussion of the way in which fiction can be used as a resource for the study of alternate sexual life-styles, see Gordon Clanton, "The Contemporary Experience of Adultery: Bob & Carol & Updike & Rimmer," in *Renovating Marriage*, Roger W. Libby and Robert N. Whitehurst, eds. (Danville, Calif.: Consensus Publishers, 1973).

[2]Jules Henry, *Pathways to Madness* (New York: Random House, 1972).

[3]Oscar Lewis, *La Vida* (New York: Random House, 1966).

[4]See, for example, Robert H. Rimmer, *Proposition 31* (New York: New American Library, 1968).

[5]See Peter L. Berger, ed., *The Human Shape of Work* (New York: Macmillan, 1964), chapter 6; and Peter L. Berger and Hansfried Kellner, "Marriage and the Construction of Reality," *Diogenes*, Summer 1964.

[6]Robert Wuthnow and Charles Y. Glock, "New Forms of Religious Consciousness Among Youth," unpublished paper (University of California, Berkeley, 1972). See also Wuthnow and Glock, "Religion, Loyalty, Defection, and Experimentation Among College Youth," *Journal for the Scientific Study of Religion,* 12:2 (June 1973), especially page 175.
From the perspective afforded by such findings, it is easier to integrate the news that former political activist Rennie Davis of the Chicago Seven is currently touring the country organizing for Guru Maharaj Ji.

[7]Our general discussion of communes is based on our own observations and upon a great deal of reading and listening. Two especially valuable resources are Rosabeth Moss Kanter, *Commitment and Community: Communes and Utopias in Sociological Perspective* (Cambridge: Harvard University Press, 1972); and Bennett M. Berger et al., "The Communal Family," *Family Coordinator* 21:4 (October 1972): 419ff.

[8]*Psychology Today*, January 1973, p. 38. See also Kathleen Kinkade, *A Walden Two Experiment: The First Five Years of Twin Oaks Community* (New York: William Morrow & Co., 1972). The question of whether communes do, in fact, constitute an effective form of political action is a valuative and semantic problem and therefore will not be addressed here.

EPILOGUE

After leaving Amy and Rich in February of 1971, Karen lived alone for about a year. During this time, she dated several men, including Brian, the man with whom she had lived prior to the group marriage arrangement. He suggested that they share an apartment, but Karen wanted some time alone to sort things out. She did not want to return uncritically to their old pattern.

In the spring of 1972, Brian moved in with Karen, and they are still living together at this writing. Karen describes their relationship as friendly and mutually supportive but lacking good sexual rapport. This Karen attributes to some health problems of Brian's. She says she does not want to get married, and he seems comfortable with this. Karen and Brian are friendly with a few other couples whom they occasionally see socially, but with none of these are they especially close.

In addition to Brian, Karen has been sexually involved with several other men since they resumed living together.

With one man in particular, she has an extremely satisfying ongoing sexual relationship that, she says, she would not give up unless it threatened her primary relationship with Brian. She clearly sees these other friendships as secondary to her life with him.

But Brian does not know about these other involvements. Karen wishes that they could discuss them together, having come to feel—as a result of her time with Rich and Amy—that candor is preferable to concealment, and that other relationships can strengthen rather than undermine a primary bond. But she knows that Brian prefers sexual exclusivity and would be threatened by her other lovers. She says she is hesitant to precipitate discussion of these issues while Brian is in poor health, but she hopes that they can be addressed in the future.

In recent months, Karen has felt "a strong, almost aching need for close women friends. . . . I have become more and more interested in the women's movement and feel a distinct need to share some of that exploration with other women." Although her one sexual experience with a woman since the end of the group marriage was "totally unsatisfactory," she is still curious about her bisexual potential and again feels that she would enjoy a sexual relationship with another female.

At work, Karen has come to resent "men who listen to my ideas only because I am wearing a low-cut dress." She wants to be seen as a competent co-worker and is learning to challenge men whose attitudes toward her abilities are affected by the fact that she is attractive. She has also come to feel that a woman must pay her own way if she wants to control her life, and so she has resumed her college education in her spare time in hopes of being promoted to a more responsible and better-paid position.

In retrospect, Karen feels that her own immaturity and her idealized perception of Amy and Rich's marriage led her to commit herself naïvely to the experiment. This also made her slow to see that it was not going to work. Based on what she knows now, she feels she could make a better go of some kind of cooperative living arrangement, and she can imagine doing so "with the right people."

For three years after the end of the group marriage, Karen had very little contact with Rich and Amy. But in recent months, communication has begun to be reestablished; correspondence and phone calls, chats with Rich, and a lunch date with Amy have loosely linked these three again. Karen is cautiously optimistic that they can be good friends.

Rich and Amy are still together. The dissolution of the group marriage was painful for them. However, they had each other and were able to return to their old pattern without much difficulty.

As before, their definition of marital fidelity allows each of them to have outside sexual and/or emotional relationships. Rich engages in sexual activity with a few women friends and participates in the swinging scene, although apparently a little less than he did before the group marriage. He says Amy and Karen helped him get in touch with his bisexual potential, and he has experienced a few homoerotic episodes. He has not, however, developed any ongoing sexual friendships with men.

Amy also has had some extramarital involvements in the past three years, but she is somewhat less active than Rich and less active than she was before Karen came to live with them. Amy has largely dropped out of swinging, preferring instead to enjoy sexual intimacy in the context of close friendships. She has renewed her relationship with Joyce and has had some rewarding erotic encounters with her, but Amy reports that, on the whole, the time with Karen has made her feel inadequate with women to such an extent that she is still somewhat reluctant to explore the sexual possibilities in her friendships with women.

Rich and Amy believe that certain unrealistic expectations

undermined the group marriage. They no longer believe complete equality and total togetherness are possible in a group living situation, and Amy fantasizes living in "a looser group marked by fewer expectations and more autonomy for each person." Amy and Rich have not forgotten the difficult times with Karen, but they smile when they remember her and their six months together. They are glad they tried.

With Karen gone, there was an extra room in the house and Amy and Rich decided to exchange that room (and board) for housekeeping and secretarial services. In the first twenty-four months after Karen's departure, five different young women lived with Rich and Amy on this basis. These women did not think of themselves as part of the family, nor were they so regarded. Rich had a brief and pleasant sexual relationship with one of them, but beyond that, these associations, although cordial, have been essentially work-centered and utilitarian.

In the spring of 1973, a young woman, Eileen, moved in under such an arrangement. Eileen was a competent typist and editor; she was also bright, pleasant, and physically attractive. In time, a warm friendship developed among the three of them; and by summer's end, Rich and Eileen were lovers—with Amy's approval, of course. On a few occasions, the three of them have made love together and, in recent months, Amy and Eileen have begun to develop a sexual relationship of their own.

Rich and Amy worked well with Eileen and enjoyed having her around. She, in turn, was fascinated by them and by their unusual marriage. She found Amy a caring friend and Rich a considerate lover who helped her learn to enjoy sex as she never had before. Gradually, Eileen moved toward their center but without seeing herself (or being seen) as a full partner. There was no talk of group marriage, as though they all sensed that to try to *name* their new arrangement might cause it to falter. They sought instead to operate without expectations, without utopian ideology.

As she came to know Amy and Rich better and learned the communications skills and ground rules that they had evolved in over a decade of being together, Eileen began to take part in probing and candid conversations with her housemates, sometimes in pairs, sometimes as three. On occasion, she served as a mediator of Rich and Amy's arguments, often supporting Amy against persistent, persuasive Rich.

In time, Eileen found herself wondering about her status in the household. She wanted to know where she fit in, and so she asked for some conscious definition of their complex association.

Amy and Rich gently resisted Eileen's request for clarification at least partly because of important issues that were taking shape between them. Amy had finished her doctorate and taken a job "working with people." Her sense of accomplishment and the discoveries she made in the lives of her clients strengthened her own self-esteem and helped her get in touch with some of her previously unexpressed (and perhaps unconscious) negative feelings toward Rich. She accused him of being bossy and selfish and of imposing his sexual rhythms on her. She named some of his defenses and even his defenses of his defenses. She took a vacation by herself for the first time in many years. She tells Rich she loves him but insists that he change. Rich, who now cooks and washes dishes one night a week, says that he *is* changing. He asks Amy to make fewer demands and to have more patience as he seeks to come to terms with this new person that his own Pygmalion proclivities have helped produce. And Amy, although she has learned to challenge Rich as she could not a few years ago, remembers how much he has helped her grow in their years together. She is concerned that she not deny him the same kind of support now.

At this writing, Rich and Amy are experiencing more conflict than during previous times in their marriage. They are not, in our judgment, fighting about issues growing out of the group marriage experiment nor about the current situation with Eileen. Both are still fully committed to and comfortable with their style of sexually open marriage. The issues around which Amy and Rich currently interact are issues that can and do arise in millions of more conventional dyads: the division of household labor, the ambiguities of male and female role expectations, the relationship between autonomy and interdependence, the development of effective communications, and trust. Sometimes they feel confident that they will resolve their differences in yet another form of unorthodox marriage. But occasionally, Amy wonders if it might not be impossible to define her own ego boundaries without separating from Rich, at least for a time.

In much that transpires between Amy and Rich these days, Eileen takes part, yet much of it she must watch from the sidelines or learn from Amy when she reports the gist of an encounter with Rich behind closed doors. Eileen knows that she must wait for the resolution of issues between Rich and Amy before her own agenda can be introduced. She seems to wish that they could resolve their differences so that the three of them could get on with the business of building a viable little community, but circumstances and the conventional wisdom push her to ask what she would do if Amy and Rich were to separate. She can imagine living with Rich in some kind of post-traditional dyad, the precise shape of which is yet to be devised. And Amy says that *if* she and Rich were to separate, she would hope that he and Eileen would stay together. "He needs somebody," she says, "and I'd feel all the more guilty if my leaving him left him *alone.*"

But Eileen has other feelings, too. "Perhaps if Rich and I live together, the same issues will come up between us that now divide him and Amy." Because she knows something of the relationship with Karen, Eileen sometimes anticipates that Rich and Amy's relationship will endure and that she will never be able to catch up. So Eileen wonders and waits. She, too, is currently planning to resume her college education, and sometimes she thinks she might like to try living alone for a while regardless of how things work out between Amy and Rich.

Unlike fiction, real stories do not end neatly when an appropriate number of words have been written and the pages filled. Like the rest of us, Amy, Rich, Karen, Eileen, and all the other people their lives touch are continuing their explorations.

BIBLIOGRAPHY

These books and articles are recommended for further exploration of questions raised by the experiment described in this volume. All may be read with profit by persons without formal training in the social sciences. Items available in paperback editions are marked with an asterisk.

*Bartell, Gilbert D. *Group Sex.* New York: New American Library, 1971. An anthropologist's study of swinging.

*Bennis, Warren G., and Slater, Philip. *The Temporary Society.* New York: Harper & Row, Publishers, 1968. Essays on changing social organization and authority patterns; pertinent to an understanding of business and government as well as the family.

Berger, Bennett M., et al. "The Communal Family," *Family Coordinator* 21:4 (October 1972): 419ff.

Berger, Peter L., and Kellner, Hansfried. "Marriage and the Construction of Reality," *Diogenes,* Summer 1964, pp. 1ff.

*Bernard, Jessie. "Infidelity: Some Moral and Social Issues." This important essay on the relationship of sexual exclusivity and permanence in marriage is reprinted in Libby and Whitehurst, eds., *Renovating Marriage,* and in Smith and Smith, eds., *Beyond Monogamy.*

*Clanton, Gordon. "The Contemporary Experience of Adultery: Bob & Carol & Updike & Rimmer." In *Renovating Marriage,* edited by Roger W. Libby and Robert N. Whitehurst. Danville, Calif.: Consensus Publishers, 1973.

*Constantine, Larry L., and Constantine, Joan M. *Group Marriage: A Study of Contemporary Multilateral Marriage.* New York: Macmillan, 1973. First study of group marriage based on extensive fieldwork and interviews.

*Cuber, John F., and Harroff, Peggy B. *Sex and the Significant Americans.* Baltimore: Penguin Books, 1966. An informative study of sexual behavior and marriage styles among the affluent.

*Gordon, Michael, ed. *The Nuclear Family in Crisis: The Search for an Alternative.* New York: Harper & Row, Publishers, 1972. Historical and cross-cultural perspectives plus analyses of some new forms of the family.

*Kanter, Rosabeth Moss. *Commitment and Community: Communes and Utopias in Sociological Perspective.* Cambridge: Harvard University Press, 1972. Comparisons of nineteenth- and twentieth-century communes.

*Kinkade, Kathleen. *A Walden Two Experiment: The First Five Years of Twin Oaks Community.* New York: William Morrow & Co., 1972. Includes discussion of this commune's beyond-Skinner approach to love, sex, friendship, and marriage.

*Libby, Roger W., and Whitehurst, Robert N., eds. *Renovating Marriage: Toward New Sexual Life-Styles.* Danville, Calif.: Consensus Publishers, 1973. Essays on alternatives to prevalent forms of intimate association.

*Lifton, Robert Jay. *History and Human Survival.* New York: Random House, 1969. The provocative essay "Protean Man" offers a portrait of a new humanity.

*Lobell, John, and Lobell, Mimi. *John and Mimi: A Free Marriage.* New York: Bantam Books, 1973. Uninhibited autobiography.

Mazur, Ronald. *The New Intimacy.* Boston: Beacon Press, 1973. Exploration of the promise and peril of open-ended marriage.

*Mead, Margaret. *Culture and Commitment.* Garden City, N.Y.: Doubleday & Company, 1970. An analysis of the generation gap, with emphasis on the ways in which young people help their parents adapt to cultural change.

*Neubeck, Gerhard, ed. *Extramarital Relations.* Englewood Cliffs, N.J.: Prentice-Hall, 1969. Essays on the forms and meanings of adultery.

*O'Neill, Nena, and O'Neill, George. *Open Marriage: A New Life Style for Couples.* New York: M. Evans & Co., 1972.

*Otto, Herbert A., ed. *The Family in Search of a Future.* New York: Appleton-Century Crofts, 1970.

*Rimmer, Robert H. *Proposition 31.* New York: New American Library, 1968. A fictional account of a two-couple group marriage.

*———. *The Rebellion of Yale Marratt.* New York: Avon Books, 1967. A fictional account of a group marriage involving one man and two women.

*Rimmer, Robert H., ed. *Adventures in Loving.* New York: New American Library, 1973. First-person accounts of experiments with group marriage.

*Skolnick, Arlene S., and Skolnick, Jerome H., eds. *Family in Transition.* Boston: Little, Brown and Company, 1971. A comprehensive reader on the family and the contemporary pressures upon it. Includes several essays on utopian forms of the family. Highly recommended.

*Slater, Philip. *The Pursuit of Loneliness.* Boston: Beacon Press, 1970. Penetrating, often partisan analysis of the counterculture. The chapter "Putting Pleasure to Work" is pertinent to discussion of the future of intimate relationships.

*Smith, James R., and Smith, Lynn G., eds. *Beyond Monogamy: Recent Studies of Sexual Alternatives in Marriage.* Baltimore: Johns Hopkins University Press, 1974. A collection of essays on swinging, group marriage, and other alternatives to conventional monogamy.

Gordon Clanton, Ph.D., is a student of human behavior and values with special interests in the intimate [sex, family, and alternative forms] and the ultimate [religions and worldviews]. He received his graduate education in religion and sociology at the Graduate Theological Union and the University of California, Berkeley. He has taught at Rutgers University and Trenton State College and has lectured and led encounter groups at colleges and growth centers.

Chris Downing holds a doctorate in Religion and Culture from Drew University. In addition to being an associate professor of religion at Rutgers University, she is president of the American Academy of Religion and a member of the board of directors of the Society for Religion in Higher Education.

Her teaching, writing, and research express her interest in depth psychology and imaginative literature; she is currently working on a study of Freud, Jung, and mythology.